Liz Gemmell

WOOLLY JUMPERS

21 easy-to-knit Australian designs

VIKING O'NEIL

Acknowledgements

So many people to thank — people who helped when I strayed out of my depth in putting this book together.

There's Leigh, my other half, who encouraged and organised me, as well as the material. And Ben, our son, who kept my pencils and textas in working order for the graphs.

There are the knitters who came to the rescue when the volume of work became overwhelming — Denise Gemmell, Edith Gemmell, Peggy Hamilton, Robyn Cox, Fran Maloney and Jenny Markey. They had to learn a new method, master it and then venture into their own efforts.

There's Bob Harris who helped with the layout; Helene Bowles who started me off, and Sue Williams who typed the manuscript at short notice.

The wonderful, patient model, Fran Miedecke, whose sense of humour got us through numerous retakes. And friends who obligingly donned jumpers — Paul Hamilton, Jane Gibbons, Annie Macnamara, Denise Stewart, Peppa Martin, Kate Maloney, and our Joe.

Finally, Gary Maloney, photographer, who managed to stay level-headed and inspired through mishaps and tiring photographic sessions, and to emerge smiling, undaunted and creative each time.

I would also like to thank the staff of David Ell Press whose invaluable help was given in so friendly a manner.

Liz Gemmell

Viking O'Neil
Penguin Books Australia Ltd
487 Maroondah Highway, PO Box 257
Ringwood, Victoria 3134, Australia
Penguin Books Ltd
Harmondsworth, Middlesex, England
Viking Penguin Inc.
40 West 23rd Street, New York, N.Y., U.S.A.
Penguin Books Canada Limited
2801 John Street, Markham, Ontario, Canada L3R 1B4
Penguin Books (N.Z.) Ltd
182–190 Wairau Road, Auckland 10, New Zealand

First published by Lloyd O'Neil Pty Ltd 1982
Revised edition 1983
Second revised edition 1984
Reprinted 1985, 1986
This edition published by Penguin Books Australia Ltd 1989
10 9 8 7 6 5 4 3 2 1

Produced by Viking O'Neil
56 Claremont Street, South Yarra, Victoria 3141, Australia
A division of Penguin Books Australia Ltd

Printed and bound in Hong Kong through Bookbuilders Limited

National Library of Australia
Cataloguing-in-Publication data

Gemmell, Liz.
   Woolly jumpers.

   2nd rev. ed.
   Bibliography.
   ISBN 0 670 90135 0.

   1. Knitting — Australia — Patterns. 2. Sweaters — Australia. I. Title.

746.9'2

Contents

Introduction

What I have tried to do is to clarify the various steps necessary to design your own jumper. With the instructions and graphs and the sections on jumper design and variations, I hope that I have given you the inspiration to work out your own patterns.

The first step is to visualise your jumper. Then sketch it until you are satisfied with the result. And finally, apply whichever rules suit the garment you have sketched.

When a knitting pattern is written, it is inevitable that it reads as the only way the garment can be made. For the sake of clarity, I have not been able to dispel this 'absoluteness' in arranging my knitting instructions. I hope that you may see variations and alternatives that I have not given and realise that these variations are possible and easy.

Needle size chart

Metric	English
10.00	000
9.00	00
8.00	0
7.50	1
7.00	2
6.50	3
6.00	4
5.50	5
5.00	6
4.50	7
4.00	8
3.75	9
3.25	10
3.00	11
2.75	12
2.25	13
2.00	14

Abbreviations

K.	knit
P.	purl
st.	stitch
sts	stitches
st. st.	stocking stitch
rem.	remaining
beg.	beginning
inc.	increase
dec.	decrease
alt.	alternate
tog.	together
yon	yarn over needle
yfwd	yarn forward

General knitting hints

Tension

Most critical to all knitting is the tension. The number of stitches to the centimetre must be the same as the instructions indicate, or your otherwise careful knitting will not produce the garment shown in the pattern.

In order to achieve this, you may have to alter the size of the needles given in the instructions. If you knit too many stitches to the centimetre, then try a size larger needle; if you knit too few stitches to the centimetre, you will need to use a size smaller needle. Keep adjusting the needle size until you can match the tension in the instructions. Using a different sized needle is of no importance. What is important is that you obtain the same number of stitches and rows as the instructions recommend.

To test your tension with a particular yarn, either the one suggested in the instructions or your own hand-spun, you should cast on 30 stitches and knit at least 10 cm in the appropriate stitch (usually stocking stitch). This will show clearly any tension differences whereas a smaller swatch would make any variation seem negligible. Don't be tempted to push or pull the swatch to the correct size.

Measure the sample in several places on a flat surface, preferably with a rigid rule rather than a flexible tape, to confirm the result. Pins may be used to mark the beginning of your count and the end.

Also take note of instructions on the label around the yarn. Often you will find a suggested number of stitches per centimetre and a suggested needle size. Use these as guides to help you.

Correcting mistakes

When you recommence work after a break, check for errors. If there is a mistake that cannot be corrected by overembroidering a knitting stitch in the correct colour (this applies to picture knitting only and not to one-colour texture patterns) then the work will need to be unravelled.

When unravelling rows containing several colours, work carefully by pulling out each colour in its sequence along the row. Don't worry about the unravelled wool tangling at this stage. Once the mistake is reached and corrected, the stitches need to be picked up. Use a size smaller needle to do this. Make sure you have picked up the correct number of stitches before you restart knitting. First and last stitches have a way of slipping down a couple of rows unnoticed. The unravelled wool can now be untangled and rewound into neat balls. Careful counting across the row will help to eliminate mistakes, but if your counting does not tally with the graph, don't assume it will correct itself. Check immediately and rectify the error at once.

Joining wool

Where possible, always tie in a new ball at the edge of a row. With picture knitting this will only be possible with the main colour, and, of course, Fair Isle. Colour changes within the row are described in the section on picture knitting.

Sewing up

To join the pieces of the garment, use a large tapestry needle with a blunt point. This will slip between the stitches easier and not pierce the wool, making it hard to pull through. You can use thinner yarn of the same colour or split the yarn with which you have been knitting. Some yarns are easy to divide and sew up well while others pull apart and break frequently. Don't waste time with the latter. Take care to change colours when necessary: a different colour showing at the seams detracts from your work.

Use a back stitch for all seams, a flat stitch for ribbed sections and a loose slip stitch for securing the neckband to the inside.

Pressing

Press each piece on the wrong side. Sometimes pinning the wool to an ironing board helps to keep the edges from rolling. Remember not to stretch the work when you are doing this. Place a damp cloth over the wool and press with an iron. Don't drag the iron across your work and don't press the ribbing. Pressing is optional especially with hand-spun yarns. The rough texture of some hand-spun has its own appeal that would be diminished with pressing.

Knitting with cotton yarn

The same general rules apply for knitting with cotton yarns as for knitting with wool. However, extra care is needed at the colour changes. At this point, correct tension is important as crossing colours over too tightly may pull the work, and in reverse, a loose tension will leave a bigger stitch.

Sometimes it may be necessary to use machine thread of a matching colour to stitch in the 'tails' as weaving them in is not always an adequate way of securing them. Cotton has a tendency to work loose.

Cotton also loses its elasticity very quickly. A few rows of shirring elastic will keep rib sections in shape and a row of shirring elastic will prevent straight necklines from eventually dropping. Use a tapestry needle and tie the ends of the elastic together, then secure them so they cannot be seen.

Crochet trim

A knit stitch crochet is particularly effective around neck openings and armholes as it can only be worked in one direction.

Knit stitch Work from right to left without turning at end of row. If necessary break off yarn and start at beginning of row again. Insert hook through work and bring out loop. Insert hook through work again and draw thread right through the stitch on crochet hook. Repeat along edge of work until circle is completed. Insert hook into top of first stitch and draw thread right through the stitch on hook. Repeat until sufficient rows are worked. Keep tension as loose or as tight as edge requires.

Knitting-stitch embroidery (or Swiss darning)

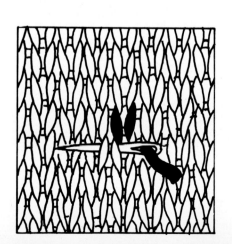

Knitting-stitch embroidery may be used for small, fiddling areas of design on your jumper. It can also be used to correct tiny errors in knitting the design that have slipped past unnoticed.

Always use a tapestry needle and the same ply yarn as for the area being worked. Keep an even tension: slightly loose is better than tight. As in knitting, each square represents one knitted stitch.

Start at the bottom right hand of the area to be worked. Bring needle from the back to the front through the centre of the stitch. Working from right to left, take the needle behind the two strands of stitch above.

Bring the needle back to the centre and behind the two strands in row below and then up through the centre of the next stitch to be worked. This completes one stitch. Continue in this way across the row for the required number of stitches.

When starting the second row, bring the needle from the back to the front through the centre of the stitch below the one to be worked. This row will be worked left to right. Pick up two strands of stitch above and bring needle back into the centre and behind the strands in row below. The needle will come up in the centre of each stitch in the previously worked row.

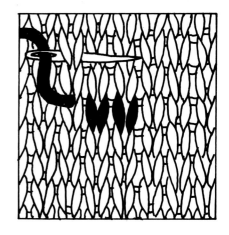

Pompons

Cut two circles of the same diameter out of cardboard. Cut two holes of the same size in each circle. The bigger the hole, the more yarn can be threaded through it. Draw the yarn through the two inner circles placed together, around the outer edge and back through the inner circle. Use manageable lengths of yarn. Keep ends of yarn to the outside of the circle. You may tie knots when joining yarn as these can be trimmed off when the pompon is finished. When no more yarn can fit through the hole, cut yarn between the two circles. Have ready a length of yarn to tie around the cut threads. Tie tightly between the cardboard circles and use the ends to attach pompon to jumper or to cord. You may have to tear the circles to remove them. Fluff up the cut ends and trim any uneven threads.

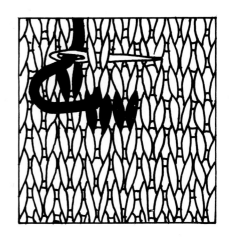

Fair Isle

Fair Isle knitting is usually done with two colours but a third colour is sometimes used. Knitting with more than three colours across a row can be cumbersome, but it is by no means impossible. It can also produce bulk at the back of the work. Colours are usually started at the beginning of a row and are carried right through to the end of the row.

Tension of Fair Isle knitting should be the same as for regular stocking stitch. Keep the threads at the back of the work loose, not tight. Tight threads will limit elasticity of the knitted garment and also create a lumpy look across the pattern. A helpful hint here is to stretch the stitches on the right hand needle (i.e. the stitches just knitted) along the needle. This allows the new colour to be brought across at a suitable tension.

At the back of the Fair Isle, one colour should always be kept above and the other colour below the row being worked. This will also help to retain elasticity and an even finish to the knitting.

If a thread is to be carried over a distance of more than five stitches, it is advisable to catch the thread in the middle. This will keep the thread along the row and prevent a long loop forming on the inside which could catch and pull when putting on or taking off the garment.

Tangles may be a problem again. Untangle the balls of yarn every so often. It is not necessary to make separate balls of colour for Fair Isle knitting. Just use the yarn as required.

Designing in Fair Isle

After knitting a swatch, you will know the number of stitches and rows in your garment. You can then start working out your own untraditional Fair Isle. Determine the number of stitches for the Fair Isle band, e.g. 80 stitches, and divide that evenly, say by eight. This means that every 10 stitches will be a single pattern which will be repeated eight times. To vary the Fair Isle, another band of a single pattern of eight stitches can be repeated 10 times. To facilitate matching up the Fair Isle when sewing the sides together, add one more stitch to either side, so that the stitches number eighty-two.

Work your pattern out on graph paper, repeating the pattern about three times to see how the design will appear along a band. Pattern sections may be of one stitch only. Remember to keep the distance between colours short, otherwise the thread at the back will need to be caught several times.

Numbers and words may be worked out in this way and knitted across as a band of Fair Isle. This can be particularly appropriate for racing, yachting, car and bike enthusiasts.

Picture knitting

Method A: Front of work

Method A: Back of work

Method B: Front of work

Method B: Back of work

Knitting pictures into jumpers is not as complicated as it appears. As in any other craft or skill there are a few rules to follow.

1 The main concern is to prevent holes appearing in your work. This is likely to happen where you need to change from one colour to another along the row. Therefore, the critical rule is always to interlock the two yarns being worked. There are two methods of doing this:

a. Put the colour you have just used on top of the one you are about to use. This brings the new colour from underneath and forms a single twist, which will prevent holes appearing at the colour change.

b. Alternatively, a double twist method can be used. Put the colour you have just used underneath the new colour and then over to the right.

With both methods, the procedure stays the same whether working across a knit or purl row, and whether progressing three or more stitches or not at all. In addition, always keep a firm, but not tight, tension when changing from one colour to another.

Determine which method suits you and soon it will become an easy habit.

2 A separate ball must be used for every colour area in your design. For example, in the Bottle-brush and Wattle jumper, there are eight sections of yellow for wattle, four medium green leaves, one large and four small sections of red and four sections of light green. You need to divide each large ball of yarn into a working number of smaller balls, otherwise you may be left with a number of half-used balls of the one colour. At times I have even counted how many stitches make up a special colour area and measured out a length of yarn. This practice is only suitable for small areas.

Once you have divided your colours into small balls, you are ready to start. Take the Bottle-brush and Wattle jumper as an example:

Row 1: Knit all main colour (m.c.) (1 ball)

Row 2: P.57 m.c., P.5 yellow, P.18 m.c. (3 balls)

Row 3: K.17 m.c., K.8 yellow, K.40 m.c., K.6 green, K.9 m.c. (5 balls)

These five balls will be used until row 9 when a new colour, yellow, is introduced, as well as one more ball of main colour. Thus row 9 will have seven balls of yarn, and so on.

3 Tangles will be inevitable. Untangle the yarn as you go. Remember that you will only be knitting with all the colours for a few rows, and then a colour will end and help to reduce the tangle.

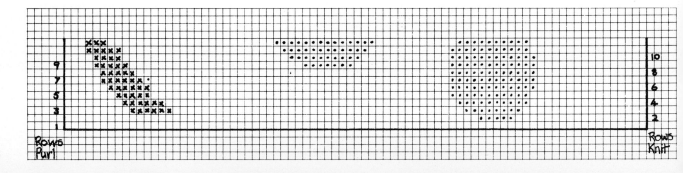

4   To join in a new colour, tie a single knot with the new colour and the yarn with which you have just knitted. Leave enough 'tail' as this will later be woven into the back of the work to secure it. Now the next stitch should be with the new colour.

With cotton yarns, leave more 'tail' as cotton has a tendency to slip, whereas wool will stay put when woven in.

5   To finish off a colour, allow sufficient yarn to tie a single knot and still leave a tail to weave in later.

If a colour finishes but starts again 10 or more stitches further along the row, you can carry it along the row as in Fair Isle technique. Keep the thread loose and catch it every five stitches at the back of the work while knitting. This thread must be loose, otherwise it will pull and not allow the knitted fabric the correct elasticity.

Use the same technique if the colour occurs again a few rows later. Otherwise, tie off the colour and start with it again as it occurs.

6   Once the jumper is complete, all loose threads have to be woven in to prevent unravelling. Weave the tails back into the loops created by the interlocking colours. A crochet hook makes the weaving simple, but a tapestry needle may also be used. Make sure the weaving does not show through to the right side.

This style of knitting creates its own interest. You can see the picture grow as you work as every row is important. In addition, colours start and finish frequently and you feel that you are making quick progress. Sometimes, you will find it impossible to put the work down until the budgie's head has been done, or until a certain colour has been completed.

The back of the work should look like this before you weave in the tails.

Reading a graph

'One picture is worth a thousand words' — a graph really fits this description. But first the words.

Each square of the graph represents a stitch and they are read from right to left (knit rows) and then from left to right (purl rows). So each row of squares is a row of stitches.

Start with the bottom row. This is always the knit row. In this book you will find an explanation of what happens if you start with a purl row first. This is done to reverse the design.

The first, third, fifth, seventh, etc. rows are knit rows and you read from right to left. The second, fourth, sixth, eighth, etc. rows are purl rows and are read from left to right.

You will find it helpful if you write down the number of each row as you start it. Use a sharp drawing pencil (easy to erase), and write the number outside the graph. By writing down the number of the row you will also know where you are up to when you need to leave your work.

Mark down, also, how many stitches are in each colour section. It saves recounting and can be erased later.

To help in counting the stitches, a grid can be ruled over the graph, say every five stitches and every five rows.

Reading increases

An extra square added to the outline of the jumper means an increase of one stitch. An extension of five or more stitches means to cast on five or more stitches at the beginning of that row. This may happen on either knit or purl rows.

Reading decreases

The deletion of a square from the outline of the jumper means a decrease

Increasing
A: Inc. 1 st. 7 times each alt. row.
B: Cast on 13 sts.
C: Cast on 10 sts 3 times each alt. row.
D: Continue straight (no further shaping).

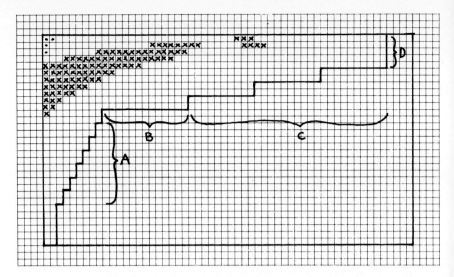

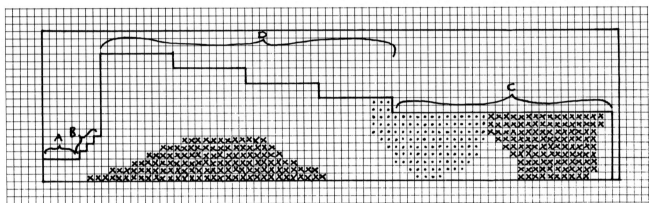

Decreasing
A: Cast off centre 14 sts (neck).
B: Dec. 1 st. every row 3 times at neck edge.
C: Cast off 30 sts.
D: Cast off 10 sts 4 times each alt. row.

of one stitch. When 10 or more squares have been deleted, this is the number of stitches to be cast off. This also occurs on either knit or purl rows.

When graphing a pattern with an odd number of stitches, as for a V-neck jumper or a special Fair Isle pattern, there will be a single centre stitch, e.g. 40 sts, 1 centre st., 40 sts. When graphing a pattern with an even number of stitches there will be a centre line dividing the stitches, e.g. 40 sts, 40 sts.

Reversing a graph

Sometimes it is necessary to reverse a design. For example, for the Wattle cardigan a right front is given and to work the left front the graph needs to be read in reverse. To match up designs at the sides, a reversed garment piece is also needed as in the Ayer's Rock and Bottle-brush and Wattle jumpers. Other designs in this book which are to be worked with a reverse design are Lorikeets, Rosella and the yoke of Possum. Snake and Boomerang could also be adapted to a garment piece worked in reverse.

Reading a graph in reverse is a simple procedure.
1 Erase any working figures you may have written on the graph.
2 Cast on and work rib section as usual.
3 First row of graph is still to be read as a knit row, but reverse the direction. This is important. Read the first row from left to right not right to left as is usual for a knit row. This means that all knit rows commence from the left-hand side and are still odd-numbered. Purl rows are read from the right-hand side but are still even-numbered. As an example, take the first four rows of the Bottle-brush and Wattle jumper. The reversing of the design would read like this:

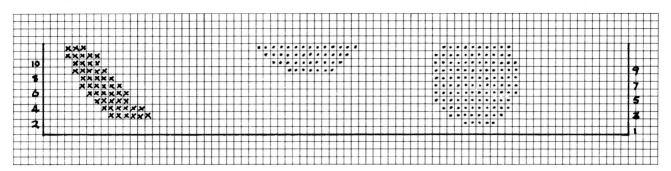

Row 1: K.80 (read from left to right).
Row 2: P.18 m.c., P.5 yellow, P.57 m.c. (right to left).
Row 3: K.9 m.c., K.6 green, K.40 m.c., K.8 yellow, K.17 m.c. (left to right).
Row 4: P.16 m.c., P.10 yellow, P.40 m.c., P.6 green, P.8 m.c. (right to left).
4   All the shaping instructions should be followed as usual. Any casting off that needs to be done should be done a row before the row shown on the graph. Decreasing by one stitch at the beginning or at the end of the row should still be carried out as indicated.

Designing a motif

There are two ways of designing your own jumper:
a.   A single motif placed on the front and/or back, e.g. Cockatoos.
b.   A design which takes in the entire jumper including sleeves and sides, e.g. Galah, Billabong.

Hints

1   Use graph paper available from newsagents/stationers, and make sure that it is not so faintly printed as to rub out when you are correcting.
2   Use a sharp drawing pencil as this is easier to erase when making corrections.
3   Remember that a knitted stitch is not a square shape: it is usually wider than it is long. This means that your design will not always appear in true proportion.
4   It is essential first to knit a swatch using the yarn and needles that you will employ in making your jumper. This will help in determining the number of stitches and rows your motif will incorporate.
5   Avoid fiddling bits in your design. These can be tedious to knit. Any unavoidable sections, e.g. birds' eyes, feet, etc., may be embroidered in later using a knitting stitch (see 'General knitting hints'). Think of your design as colour shapes, similar to appliqué designs, rather than embroidery. Shapes need to be bold and simple, otherwise the knitting process can become complicated. However, a complicated design is a challenge for some knitters.
6   Ideas for your designs can be found from many sources — children's colouring-in books, appliqué designs from craft/sewing books, magazines, photographs, etc.
7   If the photo/drawing you have decided to work from is too small, you can enlarge it quite simply. Draw a convenient square grid over the original and redraw this on to a larger grid prepared on the graph paper.

Single motif

Using the knitted swatch, determine the number of stitches and rows the design will involve. Draw this outline on to graph paper. Inside these guidelines sketch in the motif. Use curved lines as necessary. When you are

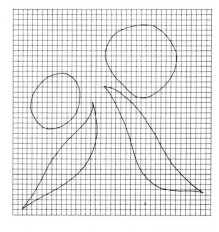

11

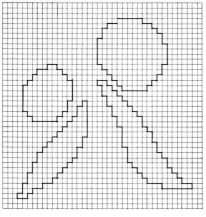

satisfied with the design, square off the curved lines and simplify the shapes if necessary. Once you have a clear outline of the shapes, you can colour in the various sections, making sure the graph lines are still visible.

Ascertain the position for the motif on your jumper. Your test swatch should give you an accurate idea of how many rows the jumper will make, so you can work out how many rows to knit before commencing the motif.

The design can be placed centrally on the jumper or it may suit to place it higher or lower and to one side, depending on the choice of design and your personal preference.

Sleeve motifs can be designed in a similar manner.

Complete jumper design

To design a motif which covers the entire jumper, you need to prepare a graph of the complete garment — body and sleeves.

If you have previously knitted a jumper that is of the size and style you prefer, you can transfer those instructions on to graph paper. This saves working out your own tension, shaping, etc., but you need to follow the instructions perfectly and not vary the yarn and tension.

However, it is not very difficult to design the complete jumper from a knitted swatch and a set of measurements. Read the sections on 'Hand-spun yarns' and 'Basic jumper design' which will show you how to use the various measurements.

Once you have prepared the graph, you can start sketching in the design. Use the same steps as described for a single motif jumper. For the complete jumper design, you are able to join the front motif to the back and to the sleeves at all the seams. In addition, as the design is all over, it is a good idea to have front and back neck openings the same. Thus there is no definite front or back to the jumper, and it can be worn either way. It makes one jumper work as two.

Note You may wish to use a graph (or part thereof) from one of the designs given in this book, but wish to change the tension or style of that particular jumper. This is possible as long as you work out your own tension and/or instructions and draw up a graph of your new version of the jumper. Then copy on to it the graph design you wish to use. The shape of the design will not vary a great deal with a new tension. You must, of course, use the same ply wool as indicated in the instructions.

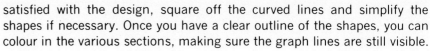

Basic jumper design

If you've already knitted and sewn up a few garments, then designing your own jumper will not be difficult at all. For a beginner in this field, the steps are simple.

A sample swatch holds the key to all the working out you need to do. Read the section on 'General knitting hints' in order to knit the sample correctly. Make sure it is wide enough and long enough, at least 15 cm wide by 20 cm long. From the sample you will derive the information you need: the number of stitches which make up 10 cm, and the number of rows which make up 10 cm.

The four rectangle jumper

Knitted fabric is soft and stretches and drapes well. These qualities allow for ease and comfort in fitting without complex shaping.

The four rectangle jumper is the simplest of all and suits a variety of ages and figures, from baby to adult sizes. There are several ways to vary this style with ribs, hems and borders, but the knitting is still simple.

Below is a chart of the body measurements you may need. To all body widths add 2 cm for a comfortable fit. Lengths may vary according to your taste and requirements.

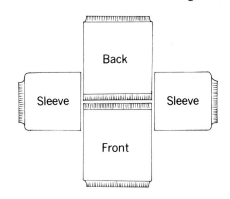

Body measurements (in cm)

Chest	55	60	65	70	75	80	85	90	95	100
Front/back width	59	64	69	74	79	84	89	94	99	104
Front/back length	35	40	44	48	52	56	62	66	70	74
Sleeve width	24	28	32	34	38	38	40	40	44	44
Sleeve length	22	27	33	38	42	42	46	46	50	50

The lengths of both front/back and sleeve may be altered. If you prefer a short sleeve or a roll-up cuff then the length will vary accordingly. A dress or tunic may also be knitted in this style by increasing the length as necessary.

METHOD

Front/back   Take the chest/bust measurement and halve it, e.g. a chest/bust measurement of 85 cm halved is 42.5 cm. Add 2 cm to this measurement for a comfortable fit, that is 44.5 cm. This measurement is the width of the two front/back pieces.

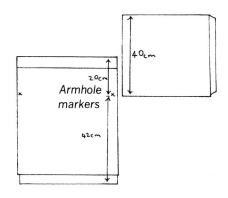

From the tension sample you have knitted, you can now work out the number of stitches and rows needed. For example, if your tension is 15 stitches to 10 cm and 20 rows to 10 cm, you will need 64 stitches to measure 42.5 cm and 124 rows to measure 62 cm.

Sleeves   Follow the same procedure for the sleeves. Note that the armhole will be marked on the front/back as half the sleeve width from the shoulder seam.

BORDERS

1 Ribbed basque   Knit this on needles which are two sizes smaller than the body needles. The basque may be between 4 cm and 8 cm in length. It may be worked in a single rib of K.1, P.1 or a double rib of K.2, P.2.

Cuff for sleeve   To knit a ribbed band for the sleeve that fits the wrist well, you need to cast on a smaller number of stitches, say about half to two-thirds of the total number. Use small needles and work in rib for desired length. Change to body size needles and increase evenly along next row till total number of stitches is reached. Knit the required length and cast off loosely. The sleeve will appear as though gathered into the cuff.

Neckline   The neckline rib may be knitted on the same needles as the body as this will allow extra stretch along the shoulder line. Alternatively, use the smaller needles for a firmer rib. In either case, cast off very loosely in rib. Loose casting off is important, otherwise the rib neckline will not fit over the wearer's head. In order to cast off loosely, use a needle two to four sizes larger than the right-hand needle. Should the neckline prove too large or lose its elasticity after a time, thread a row or two of shirring elastic through the neckline rib. Secure at a shoulder seam so the elastic is not visible.

2 Moss stitch border   If a straight look is required, then a ribbed band is unsuitable. Moss stitch creates a firm, non-roll border and looks attractive. Use small needles for moss stitch. Cast on an odd number of stitches. K.1, P.1 to last stitch, K.1. Work this pattern for each row.

3 Garter stitch border   Garter stitch creates a ridged border that stands out from the stocking stitch of the body and sleeve. Every row is worked in knit stitches. Use smaller needles than for the body of the garment.

4 Hemmed edges   A hem will give a tailored finish. Use small needles when knitting a hem. Work 5 cm in stocking stitch finishing with right side facing. Next row, purl to form a ridge fold line. Change to body needles, and beginning with a purl row, work in stocking stitch as required. On completion, sew up side seams and then slip stitch hem to body.

All these borders can also be used for the sleeves. Note that the sleeve will hang straight and not gather in as for the ribbed cuff.

SEWING UP

To form the neckline, join 8 cm, or less for small sizes, at shoulders. Use a flat seam for all ribbed basques.

Sew in sleeve using a back stitch with armhole markers as guides. Sew up side and sleeve seam.

GRAPHING

The four rectangle jumper is very easy to graph. One stitch is one square and a row of squares is a row of stitches. Once you have drawn up the width (stitches) and length (rows) you can incorporate the design of your choice.

Jumper variations

Shaped sleeve

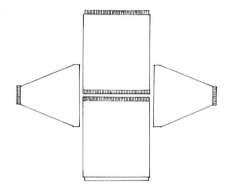

This is a simple variation on the basic four rectangle jumper design. The front/back pieces remain the same, only the sleeve is shaped from the cuff, which can still be worked in any of the four borders or basques.

The cuff is usually two-thirds or one-half of the final sleeve width. Increase one stitch at each end of every fourth, sixth or eighth row until correct number of stitches is acquired to suit the sleeve width. The rate of increase depends on the length of the sleeve, and is worked out from the number of rows that make up the sleeve. If the maximum number of stitches is reached and the length of the sleeve is still too short, work the extra rows with no shaping. Cast off loosely.

Shaped sleeve top

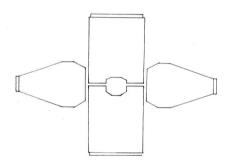

The shaped sleeve top gives a comfortable fit to the shoulder/armhole. It does not need to be set into an armhole. Armhole markers can be used simply as guides. The shaped top length is not critical and is not as deep as a proper set-in sleeve. Usually a convenient number of stitches is cast off each row and then the remaining stitches are cast off. For example, if the sleeve measures 60 stitches in width, then 6 stitches could be cast off at the beginning of the next 8 rows and then 12 stitches cast off once. This shaping gives sufficient 'rise' to the sleeve to facilitate a comfortable fit.

Shoulder shaping

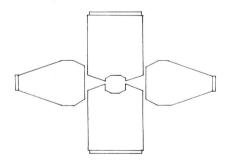

Shoulder shaping gives a tailored line to the garment. Take one-third of the stitches for the body and work out a comfortable decrease over three alternate rows. For example, if 20 stitches make up a third of the total body width, then a comfortable decrease could be: cast off 7 stitches at beginning of next 2 rows and 6 stitches once. For the left shoulder the casting off occurs on knit rows, and for the right shoulder, on purl rows.

Armhole shaping

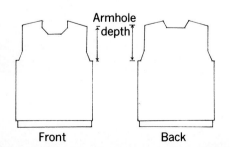

Armhole
depth

Front   Back

A set-in sleeve and a shaped armhole should be designed together as both rely on the same measurement. This measurement is the depth of the armhole. For a comfortable fit, the armhole should begin level with the chest and end on the shoulder. This measurement is taken in a straight line and is shown as a straight line on the pattern or graph. An armhole that begins higher up, closer to the armpit, will fit too snugly once the sleeve is set in. This is desirable for jumpers that follow the body line. I have chosen a looser, more casual line as this allows for more design flexibility and ease in fit.

The shaping is achieved by casting off 4 stitches (more or less) at the beginning of the next 2 rows. The casting off may be repeated once more to create a square-shaped armhole. More gradual shaping results from decreasing 1 stitch at each end of every alternate row until required shaping is reached. Continue straight till shoulder shaping begins. The straight side of the armhole edge should line up with the wearer's shoulder.

Set-in sleeve

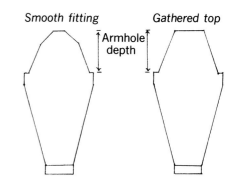

Once the armhole depth is determined, the sleeve top can be shaped to accommodate this measurement. Work sleeve until underarm length has been reached. Initial armhole shaping begins by casting off an equivalent number of stitches as for armhole on front/back. Then one stitch is decreased at each end of every alternate row and, when necessary, every row, until armhole depth is reached. The final stitches are then cast off. If this number is large then a gathered sleeve top results. If a fitted sleeve top is required then decreases must occur more frequently, i.e. decrease every row.

Neckline

The neckline is in the centre third of the front/back and is 7 cm deep. If a definite back is required, the neckline needs to be only 4 cm deep at the back to make it higher than the front.

If you are preparing a graph of the jumper, you need to know the number of rows for the front/back. This will tell you where to start the neckline shaping, and how many rows the 7 cm neckline will take. In terms of measurement, it is simple to work out. For example, if the length of the front/back is 62 cm, then the neck shaping will begin at 55 cm. For the back, the neck shaping will begin at 58 cm.

The width of the neck opening is one-third of the total stitches for the front/back. For example, if the front/back is 60 stitches in width, then the neck opening will be 20 stitches wide. Shaping may be worked in this way: cast off the centre 10 stitches (half of the total number of neck opening), then decrease 1 stitch at neck edge every alternate row or every row 5 times. Work straight till depth of neckline measures 7 cm. Join yarn at centre to remaining stitches and complete other side to correspond.

The neckline may be widened or deepened depending on the style you wish to create.

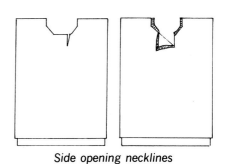
Front   Back

NECKLINE STYLES

The crew neck is a popular, easy-to-wear style.

A set of four needles is needed to knit the crew neck ribbing in the round. If one shoulder is sewn up, then crew neck ribbing is knitted with two needles. On completion of ribbing, the remaining shoulder seam is sewn up and the ribbing is joined.

Use needles two sizes smaller than for body knitting, and with right side of work facing, pick up a comfortable even number of stitches. Pick up the stitches loosely, otherwise the head may not fit through the neck opening. Rib 6–10 cm in length then cast off loosely in rib. The neckband is then folded in half and slip-stitched loosely to the inside.

Side opening necklines

Alternatively, a polo neck can be worked along the same lines. The length of the neckband in this case is usually about 15 cm, but would vary according to the size of the jumper and taste.

A cowl neckline is achieved by designing a wider neckline for the jumper. Pick up the stitches for the cowl collar and rib or work in stocking stitch for 30 cm. Cast off loosely in rib. If collar has been worked in stocking stitch, work four rows of knit to prevent curling, and cast off loosely. Remember, if working a cowl collar in stocking stitch, start with a purl row and then a knit row, otherwise the stocking stitch will not appear on the correct side.

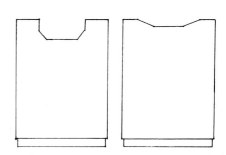

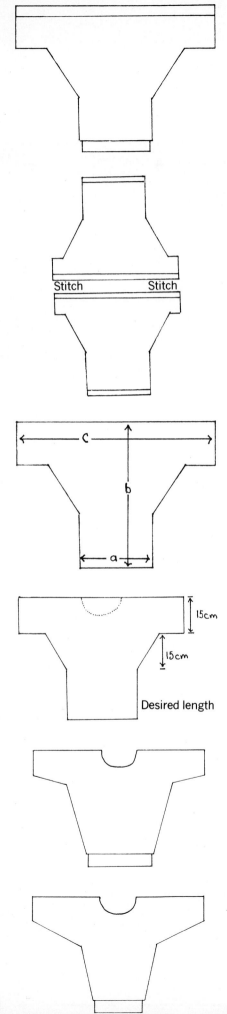

The dolman sleeve jumper

For a basic dolman sleeve jumper, two pieces are worked the same for the front and the back. The edge forming the sleeve and head opening may be several rows of rib or garter stitch. In either case casting off should be loose. Stitch along the shoulder line from sleeve edge and leave an opening large enough to go over the head, or larger if a wider neckline is preferred.

When knitted in cotton the neckline will drape more than when knitted in wool. Thus, if a round neckline is desired when working in wool, it must be designed into the garment piece (see 'Variations on the four rectangle jumper').

Measurements

You need three measurements:

a.   Width of front/back which is half of chest measurement plus 2 cm for ease.

b.   Length from shoulder line to bottom of garment.

c.   Width across shoulder line from sleeve edge to sleeve edge.

From the tension swatch you have knitted with the intended yarn, you will be able to work out how many stitches to cast on and how many rows long the garment will be.

Extended sleeve

The extended sleeve shaping begins 15 cm beneath a regular armhole. The increase is usually worked thus: increase 1 stitch at each end of every alternate row until desired shaping has been achieved. Finish off by casting on from 2 to 5 stitches at the beginning of the next 2 rows.

To finish off the extended sleeve you may either work a ribbed band or several rows of slip stitch crochet.

Dolman sleeve

The dolman sleeve jumper is very similar to the extended sleeve jumper except that the shaping increase begins earlier. The extended shaping usually begins a few centimetres above waist level or right at waist level. The shaping continues to 5 cm below the regular armhole. Then the sleeve is made by casting on 10 stitches (or more) every row till desired length is achieved. The shoulders need not be shaped. After the neckline has been completed, the whole row of shoulder stitches may be cast off.

A dolman sleeve jumper requires a large number of stitches which can become cumbersome to handle. Don't be deterred: a circular needle simplifies knitting with a large number of stitches. They allow for the incorporation of interesting motifs and, of course, there are only two garment pieces to knit, not four.

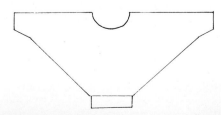

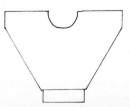

Woolly jumpers

If you can knit plain and purl and like to play around with colour, then these jumpers are for you. The knitting is easy, the shapes and directions are simple, and the colour is fun. Read the instructions first on how to make colour changes and how to read graphs and you have all the pre-requisites for this type of knitting.

I have tried to keep to the true colours of the birds, animals and flowers as I have seen them in the wild or in photographs. But there is still scope for your own colour choice of background colour as this can effectively change the character of the whole jumper.

Some graphs are in black and white. To help to recognise the colours and shapes more easily, colour in the graph yourself with pencils so that the graph lines are still visible and easy to count.

Other chapters in this book will tell you how to achieve different effects by substituting other yarns for those suggested. Bead and leather trims may also be added as you wish.

Christmas Bells

Colour makes this jumper vibrant. The flowers and birds are bright but the blue accentuates the colours. A big jumper to fit almost any size.

Materials
Cleckheaton 12 ply wool 50 gm balls
13 balls blue (m.c.)
4 balls red
3 balls yellow
2 balls black
1 ball apple green
1 pair 5.5m needles
1 pair 8.0m needles

Measurement

To fit up to 97 cm chest/bust.

Tension
12 sts to 10 cm over st. st. using 8.0m needles (or whichever needles will give the correct tension).

☐	☐	Blue (m.c.)
1	■	Red
2	■	Yellow
3	■	Black
4	■	Green

Front and back
Using 5.5m needles and m.c., cast on 64 sts. Rib (K.1, P.1) 12 rows. Change to 7.5m needles and work from graph.
Armholes   At row 65, cast off 6 sts, and again at following row. Work 28 rows without shaping.
Shoulders   Cast off 7 sts at beg. of next 4 rows. Graph ends here. Work from written instructions.

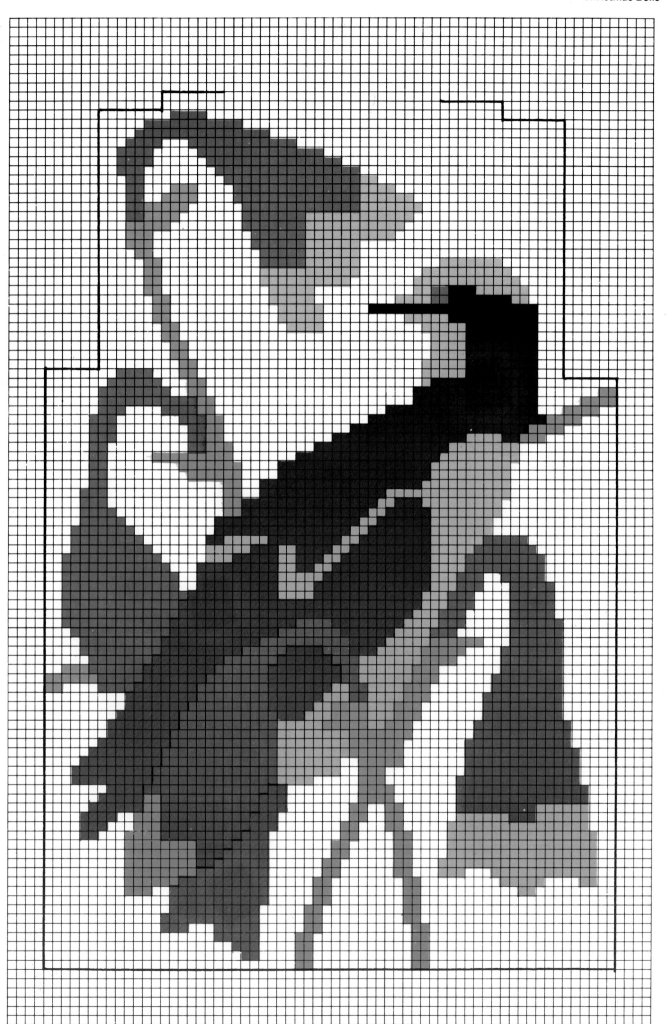

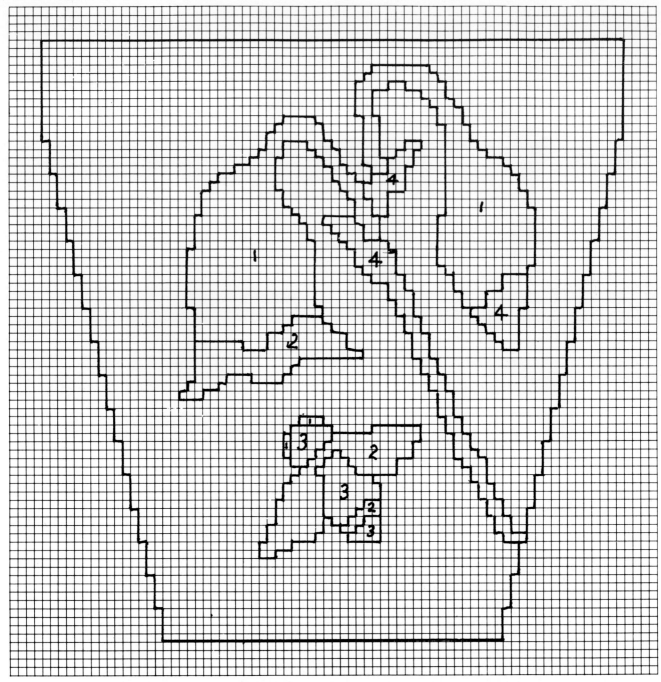

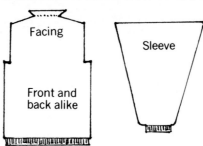

Facing

Front and
back alike

Sleeve

Neck   Work 4 rows of st. st., dec.
1 st. at each end of knit rows. Work
next row in purl to mark neck fold
line.
Facing   Work 4 rows in st. st., inc.
1 st. at each end of every K. row.
Cast off very loosely.

Sleeves
Using 5.5m needles and m.c., cast
on 36 sts. Rib (K.1, P.1) for 11
rows. On 12th row inc. 6 sts. evenly
along row. Change to 7.5m needles

and commence working from
graph. Inc. 1 st. at each end of 5th
row and thereafter every 4th row
till 72 sts. Work 11 rows without
shaping. Cast off.

Note
Bee may be omitted from second
sleeve.

To make up
Join shoulder seams using back st.
Fit cast-off edge of sleeve to
armhole. Sleeve top may need to be
slightly gathered to fit armhole.
Back st. sleeve in place, making
sure corner of sleeve is stitched to
armhole shapings. Stitch up sleeve
and side seams. Turn neck facing
to inside and slip st. into position.
Secure facings to shoulder seams.
Weave in all loose threads along
colour changes.

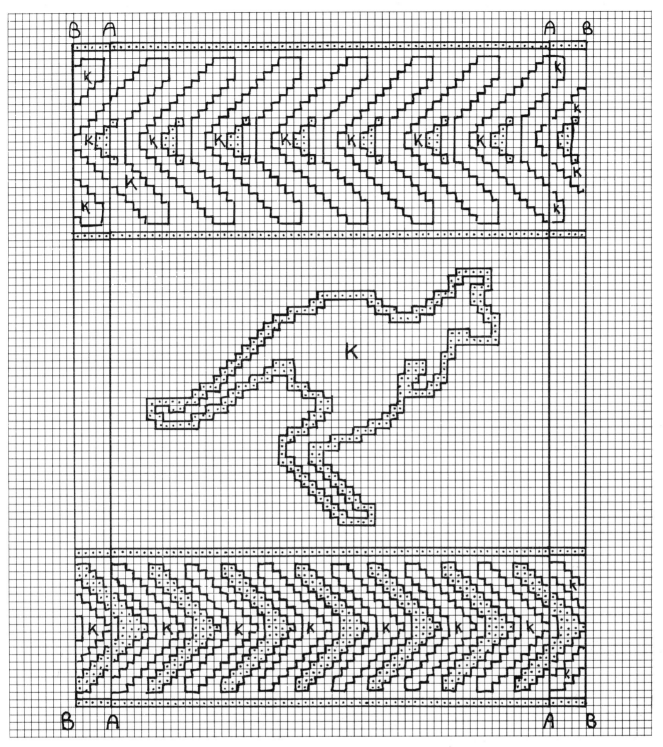

Kangaroo and Boomerang

A simple design that looks attractive on men or women. The design could be easily adapted to hand-spun yarns in their natural colours. Check your tension first if using other yarns.

Materials
Patons 12 ply Winter Wool 50g balls
11, 13 balls tan (m.c.)
3 balls brown
2 balls natural white
1 pair 5.5m needles
1 pair 7.5 needles

Measurement
To fit:
A   92 cm chest/bust
B   102 cm chest/bust

Tension
Using Husky and 7.5m needles, 12 sts to 10 cm over st. st.

Note
Where there is only one figure, this applies to both sizes.

☐ Tan (m.c.)

· Natural white

K Brown

Front and back
Both alike.
Using 5.5m needles and m.c., cast on 60, 70 sts. Rib (K.1, P.1) for 10, 15 rows. Change to 7.5m needles and commence working from graph. The two bands of boomerangs are worked in Fair Isle technique where yarn is carried over at the back of work. The kangaroo is worked in the picture

21

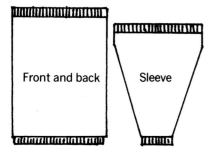

technique using separate balls for each colour section.
On completion of graph, right side

facing, work 1 knit row in tan, then work 10, 15 rows in rib (K.1, P.1) using same needles. Cast off loosely in rib.

Sleeves
Using 5.5m needles and m.c., cast on 38, 44 sts. Rib (K.1, P.1) for 10, 15 rows. Change to 7.5m needles and work in st. st. Inc. 1 st. at each end of 7th row and then every 6th row till 52, 56 sts. On this row commence graph of larger boomerangs as shown for body of jumper. Continue increasing as before until 58, 62 sts, keeping Fair

Isle pattern as established. Continue straight till Fair Isle pattern is complete. Right side of work should be facing. Work 1 knit row, then 10, 15 rows in rib (K.1, P.1) using same needles. Cast off loosely in rib.

To make up
Making a flat seam sew up 15 sts of neckline rib to form both shoulder seams. With back st. sew in sleeves using Fair Isle pattern as armhole opening. Sew up side and sleeve seams. Weave in loose threads. Press.

Bottle-brush and Wattle

Materials
Patons Family 12 ply wool 50 gm balls
14 balls navy blue (m.c.)
Patons 12 ply Winter Wool 50 gm balls
1 ball green
Patons 7 ply Flair 50 gm balls
2 balls red (use 2 strands throughout)
2 balls pale yellow
Patons Family 8 ply wool 25 gm balls
4 balls yellow
N.B. Use 1 strand of yellow mohair and 1 strand of yellow wool throughout.
Measurement
To fit up to 98 cm chest/bust.
Tension
16 sts to 10 cm over st. st. using 6.0m needles.

Note

Front and back are alike except for the motif instructions. One side must be a reversal of the other so that the design will meet up correctly at the shoulder and at the sides. (Refer to special instructions for reversing a graph.)

☐ Navy blue (m.c.)

1 Red

2 Grey–green

3 Yellow

4 Olive green

Front

Using 4.5m needles and m.c., cast on 80 sts and rib (K.1, P.1) for 14 rows. Change to 6.0m needles and work from graph.
Row 75: Put in coloured thread markers to indicate armhole.
Row 103: Cast off centre 28 sts. Decrease 1 st. at neck edge for the following 5 rows, then every alt. row 5 times until there are 15 sts remaining. Cast off. Join yarn to remaining stitches and complete other side.

Back

As for front, but design must be reversed. The bottle-brush should be on the left shoulder. Commence graph with a knit row but read from left to right. Next row is purl but read from right to left. Neck shaping remains the same.

Sleeves

Using 4.5m needles and m.c., cast on 40 sts. Rib (K.1, P.1) for 15 rows. Row 16, increase 10 sts evenly along row (50 sts). Change to 6.0m needles and work in st. st. Increase 1 st. at each end of 5th row and then every 6th row until 80 sts. Work 6 more rows (or length required).
To shape, cast off 6 sts at beginning of following 10 rows. Cast off remaining 20 sts.

Collar

Join bottle-brush shoulders with back st. Using 4.5m needles and m.c., with right side of work facing, start at open shoulder and pick up 144 sts evenly (72 sts each section). Rib (K.1, P.1) for 22 rows.

Row 23: K.1, P.1, K.2 tog., * K.1, P.1, K.1, P.1, K.2 tog., repeat from * to end, K.1, P.1.
Row 24: K.1, P.1, * yon. K.1, K.1, P.1, K.1, P.1, repeat from * to end, K.1, P.1.
Next row: Cast off very loosely.

To make up

Use flat seam to join all rib sections including collar. Back stitch remaining shoulder seam. Sew sleeves in using coloured thread markers as guides. Sew up sleeve and side seams, taking care to change yarns when matching up wattle sections.

Cord

Using olive green, crochet a cord 100 cm long. Thread this through collar. Make 2 pompons (6 cm and 7.5 cm diameter) from yellow mohair. Attach to cord.

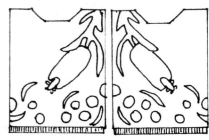

Front and back

Sleeve

Tiwi

Named after Aboriginal designs from Bathurst and Melville Islands. Translated into Fair Isle knitting technique, the design becomes symmetrical, but the Aboriginals have no need for such order. This jumper may also be knitted in hand-spun yarns in natural fleece colours (or two natural colours and a vegetable-dyed colour). Check your tension first to adapt this design to different yarns.

Materials
Patons 12 ply Winter Wool 50g balls
13, 15, 16 balls brown (m.c.)
3 balls gold
Patons Flair 25 gm balls
4 balls white (use 2 strands throughout)

1 pair 5.5m needles
1 pair 7.5m needles

Measurement
To fit:
A   60–76 cm chest/bust
B   76–92 cm chest/bust
C   92–102 cm chest/bust

☐ Brown (m.c.)

☒ Gold

⊡ White mohair

▣ White mohair bobble

Tension

12 sts to 10 cm using Husky and 7.5m needles over st. st.

Note

1   The jumper shown in the photograph is a longer fashion length. For a more conventional length, begin Fair Isle pattern at C level, omitting white section. For child's length start at A level. All lengths do *not* include 10 rows of ribbing. If you prefer to include the white section at the bottom for lengths A or C, after working the ribbed basque work 5 rows of white pattern as shown in rows 61–65 inclusive. Then begin graph from desired level.
2   The brown yarn will be worked across to the end of each row. The gold and white yarns will be worked only in the centre 40 sts, thus each will need to be given a *double* twist at either end of the panel to prevent holes occurring in the wool.
3   When only one figure is given, this refers to all sizes.

Bobble

See bobble instructions for Billabong jumper, but do not break off white yarn. It may be carried across the row.

Front and back

Alike. Using 5.5m needles and m.c., cast on 52, 60, 70 sts. Work 10 rows of rib (K.1, P.1). Change to 7.5m needles and begin at desired

length level working in Fair Isle.
Armhole   Inc. 1 st. at each end of every alt. row 4, 5, 5 times as shown on graph. Then continue without shaping for 15, 15, 16 rows. On completion of graph, work 1 row knit in m.c. and then 19 rows of rib (K.1, P.1) with the same needles (7.5m). Cast off very loosely in rib.

Sleeves

Using 5.5m needles and m.c., cast on 30, 38, 38 sts. Rib (K.1, P.1) for 10 rows. Change to 7.5m needles.
Size A only: Inc. 8 sts evenly along 1st row (38 sts).
All sizes: Inc. 1 st. at each end of 5th row and then every 6th row until 56, 58, 60 sts. Continue straight till desired length is worked. Cast off loosely.

To make up

Making a flat seam, sew up 20 sts of neckline rib to form shoulders. Sew in sleeves. Sew up side and sleeve seams using back stitch.

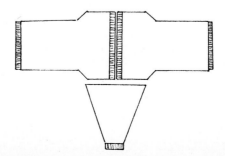

Billabong

The circle and bobbles have been adapted from an Aboriginal design for a billabong, while the elbow and waist stripes are reminiscent of body decoration used for corroborees.

Materials

Patons 12 ply Winter Wool 50 gm balls

or

Cleckheaton Landscape 50 gm balls
6, 7 balls main colour (m.c.)
5 balls contrast 2 (c.2)
3 balls contrast 1 (c.1)
1 pair 6.0m needles
1 pair 7.5m needles

Measurement

To fit:
A   80–85 cm chest/bust
B   90–95 cm chest/bust

Tension

13 sts to 10 cm using 7.5m needles over st. st.

Note

Where only one figure is given, this refers to both sizes.

Bobble

All bobbles are made with teal wool. There is no need to break off main colour.
Join in c.1, K.1 into stitch required, then slip it back on to the left-hand needle. Knit into front and back of this st. to make 5 sts. Turn work, P.5. Turn, K.5. Turn, P.5. Turn, right side facing, slip next 4 sts knitwise on to right-hand needle and knit 5th st. With left-hand needle pass 1st, 2nd, 3rd, 4th sts over 5th st. and off needle. Break off c.1, tie ends together and continue with main colour.

Back

Using 6.0m needles and c.2, cast on 60, 68 sts. Rib (K.2, P.2) for 20 rows. Jumper can be lengthened at this stage. Change to 7.5m needles and work from graph.
Size A: Put in coloured thread markers at row 51 to indicate armholes.

Billabong

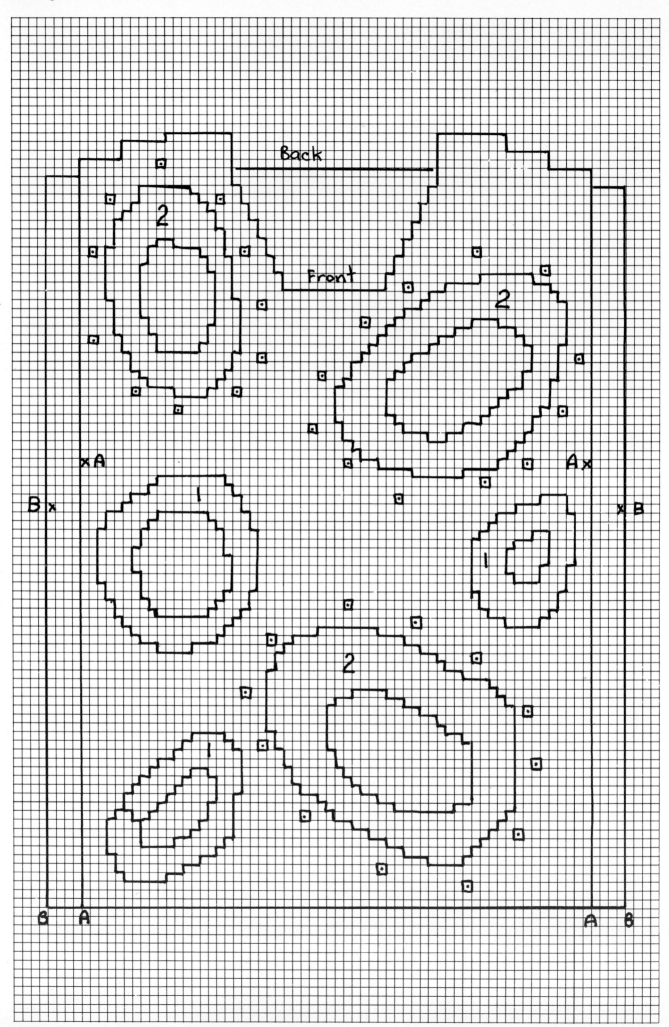

28

Size B: Put in coloured thread markers at row 45 to indicate armholes.

Shoulder shaping *Size B only:*
Cast off 4 sts at beg. of rows 83 and 84.

Both sizes: At row 85 cast off 5 sts, K.13, cast off 24 sts, K.18 to end. Cast off 5 sts at beg. of next row and alt. row. Cast off final 8 sts. Join yarn to rem. sts and complete other side to correspond.

Front

As for back until row 70. Next row, cast off centre 12 sts, work to end of row. At neck edge dec. 1 st. each alt. row 6 times.

Size A: Work 2 rows straight then cast off 5 sts at beg. of next and alt. rows, 8 sts once.

Size B: Cast off at beg. each row 4 sts once, 5 sts twice, 8 sts once. Join yarn to rem. sts and complete other side to correspond.

Sleeves

Using 6.0m needles and c.2, cast on 36 sts. Rib (K.2, P.2) for 10 rows. If necessary, lengthen sleeve at this stage. Start sleeve shaping after desired lengthening has been completed. Change to 7.5m needles and continue in rib pattern. Inc. 1 st. at each end of 5th row and then every 6th row until 58 sts. At the same time, at 48 sts change to c.1, and st. st., and work 3 rows. Change to m.c. and work from graph. When 58 sts are on needle work 6 rows

straight, then commence shoulder shaping. Cast off 4 sts at beg. of next 2 rows, then 5 sts at beg. of next 6 rows. Cast off 20 sts.

To make up

Join one shoulder. Using 6.0m needles and c.2, and with right side facing, pick up 78 sts evenly for neckband. Rib (K.2, P.2) for 20 rows. Cast off loosely in rib. Join remaining shoulder and neckband. Fold neckband in half and slip st. to inside. Sew in sleeves, stretching slightly to fit for size B. Sew side and sleeve seams.

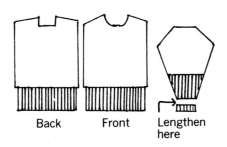

Back   Front   Lengthen here

☐	m.c.
·	Bobble
I	c.1
2	c.2

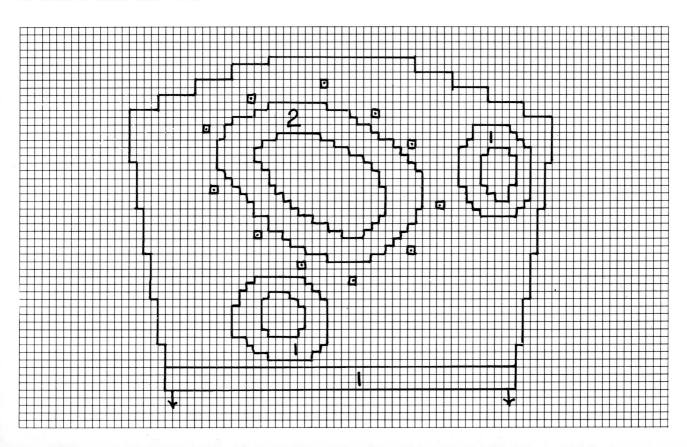

Ayers Rock

A landscape jumper for either a man or a woman. The strong colour of the rock is important because of the asymmetrical design. Balance the rock colour with strong cloud tones.

- ☐ Sky blue
- ☐ Royal blue

- ☐ Teal blue
- ☐ Gold
- ☐ Variegated
- ☐ Rust
- ☐ Green
- ☐ Navy blue

30

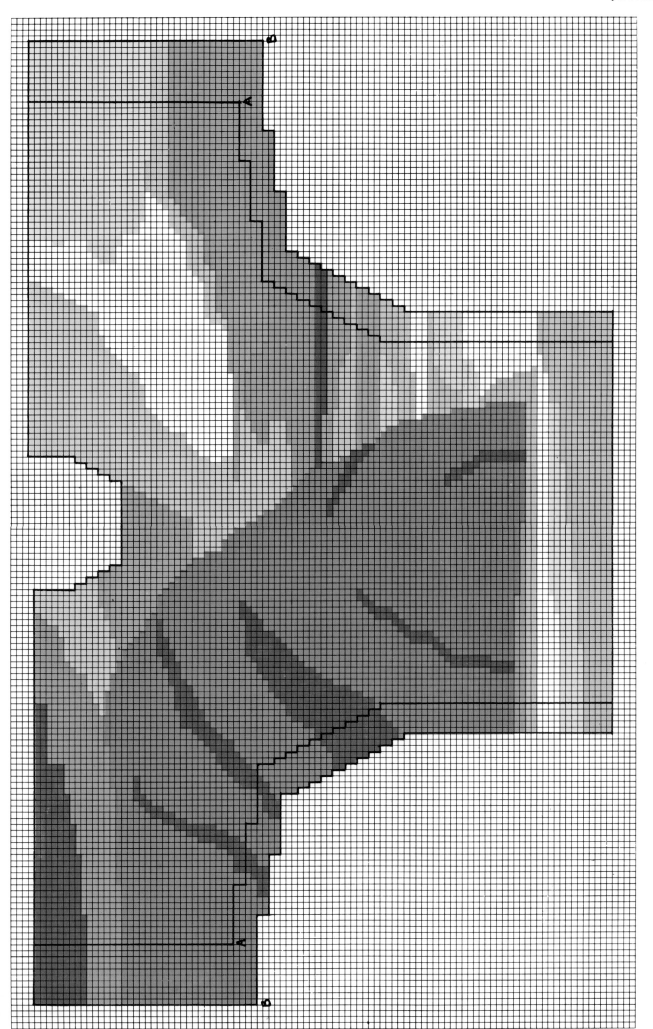

Materials

Cleckheaton 12 ply wool 50 gm balls
3 balls sky blue
2 balls deep blue
2, 3 balls teal
1 ball gold
3, 4 balls rust
1 ball navy blue
Patons Family 12 ply wool 50 gm balls
2 balls variegated white/grey
3, 4 balls green
1 pair 5.5m needles
1 pair 7.5m needles

Measurements

To fit:
A 76–92 cm chest/bust
B 92–102 cm chest/bust

Tension

12½ sts to 10 cm using 7.5m needles over st. st.

Note

Where only one figure is given, this refers to both sizes.

Front and back

Both pieces are the same. However, one piece must be reversed to allow the design to meet at the side seam. To reverse the graph, work the first row in knit as usual but read from left to right. Second row is purl but read from right to left. (See detailed instructions on reversing a graph.) Using 5.5m needles and green yarn, cast on 60, 70 sts and rib (K.1, P.1) for 10 rows. Change to 7.5m needles and work in st. st.
Size A: Commence working from graph.
Size B: Work 10 rows with green in st. st. and then commence working from graph.
Note These 10 rows are not shown on the graph, but are included in all instructions for Size B.
Dolman shaping   Begin shaping at row 41 for Size A and row 47 for

Size B. Inc. 1 st. at each end of this and every alt. row 10 times. Then cast on 10 sts at beg. of next 6 rows for Size A, 4 rows for Size B. *Size B only:* Cast on 15 sts at beg. of next 2 rows (140, 160 sts). Continue working from graph with no further shaping until row 85 for Size A, row 95 for Size B.
Neck shaping   Cast off centre 14 sts. Dec. 1 st. at neck edge 4 times. Work 7 more rows. Cast off. Join yarn to rem. sts and work to correspond.

To make up

Sew up one shoulder seam in back st. Using 5.5m needles and sky blue yarn, with right side facing, pick up 80 sts. Rib (K.1, P.1) 26 rows. Cast off loosely. (Alternatively, sew up both shoulders and use a set of four 5.5m needles.) Sew rem. shoulder seam. Fold neckband in half and slip st. to inside.

Cuffs

Rock cuff   Using 5.5m needles and rust wool, with right side facing, pick up 8, 12 sts at rock edge. Join in royal blue and pick up 8 sts, join in navy blue and pick up 8 sts, join in royal blue again and pick up 8 sts, join in rust again and pick up 8, 12 sts (40, 48 sts). Rib (K.1, P.1) for 12 rows keeping colour changes vertical. Cast off in rib.
Sky cuff   Using 5.5m needles and teal yarn, with right side facing, pick up 8, 12 sts at teal sky. Join in gold and pick up 24 sts, join in teal again and pick up 8, 12 sts (40, 48 sts). Rib (K.1, P.1) for 12 rows keeping colour changes vertical. Cast off in rib.

To make up

Use flat st. for rib sections and back st. for other seams. Sew up side seams. Weave in loose threads.

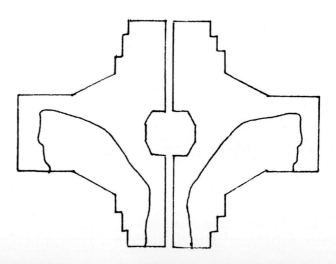

Lorikeets

Blue (m.c.)
· Yellow
X Leaf green
∧ Sunset pink

Wattle and gum blossoms frame the lorikeets. The birds are knitted with separate balls of colour, while the floral bands are worked in Fair Isle.

Materials
Patons Totem 8 ply 50 gm balls
5 balls blue (m.c.)
1 ball leaf green
1 ball pink
1 ball royal blue
small quantity red
Patons Family 8 ply wool 25 gm balls
2 balls yellow
2 balls green
Cleckheaton 8 ply wool 25 gm balls
2 balls orange
1 pair 3.75m needles
1 pair 4.5m needles
6 buttons

Measurements
Garment measures:
Chest: 72 cm
Length (back neck to hem): 55 cm
Underarm sleeve: 28 cm
The jacket will fit a child between 6–9 months and four years. Fold under sleeve to fit the baby and let down as necessary.

Tension
23 sts to 10 cm using 4.5m needles and Patons Totem over st. st.

Right front
Using 3.75m needles and m.c., cast on 42 sts. Work in st. st. for 13 rows. Knit next row to form fold line for hem. Change to 4.5m needles and work first 14 rows of Fair Isle pattern arranged thus: last 3 sts of pattern, 4 repeats of 9 st. pattern, first 3 sts of pattern. Then work from graph. On completion of graph begin Fair Isle pattern.
Raglan shaping   Cast off 4 sts at beg. of row 4 of Fair Isle. Keeping pattern correct dec. 1 st. at armhole edge next and every alt. row. At the same time begin neck shaping on row 17 of Fair Isle pattern.
Neck shaping   Cast off 6 sts at row 17 and dec. 1 st. at neck edge every alt. row till 3 sts remain. Work 2 rows, K.3 tog. Fasten off.

Left front
As for right front but reverse graph. Fair Isle pattern and raglan and neck shaping instructions remain the same but occur on opposite sides. Refer to section on 'Reversing a graph' for more details.

Back
Using 3.75m needles and m.c., cast on 69 sts. Work as for right front. Fair Isle pattern is arranged thus: last 3 sts of pattern, 7

repeats of 9 st. pattern, first 3 sts of pattern. Then work from graph. On completion of graph begin Fair Isle pattern.
Raglan shaping   On row 3 of Fair Isle pattern, cast off 4 sts at beg. of next 2 rows. Dec. 1 st. at each end of every alt. row until 25 sts rem. Work 1 row, cast off.

Sleeves
Using 3.75m needles and m.c., cast on 42 sts. Work hem as for right front. Change to 4.5m needles and inc. 1 st. at each end of this row and every 6th row until 60 sts. At the same time beg. working from graph. Work raglan shaping as for back until 20 sts rem. Dec. 1 st. at each end of next row and every row until 12 sts rem. Cast off.

Hood
Using 4.5m needles and m.c., cast on 69 sts. Work 2 rows m.c., then last 21 rows of Fair Isle pattern, 2 rows m.c., complete Fair Isle pattern, 2 rows m.c., 2 rows pink, 2 rows m.c. Cast off. Fold hood in half and flat sew cast-off edges together. Beginning at cast-on edge, with 3.75m needles and right

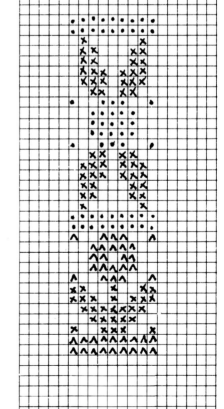

9 st. repeat pattern

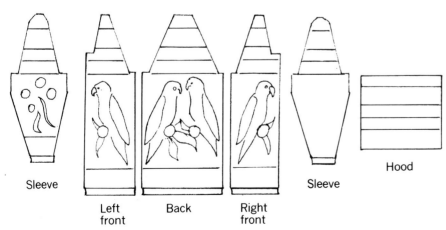

Sleeve   Sleeve

Left front   Back   Right front   Hood

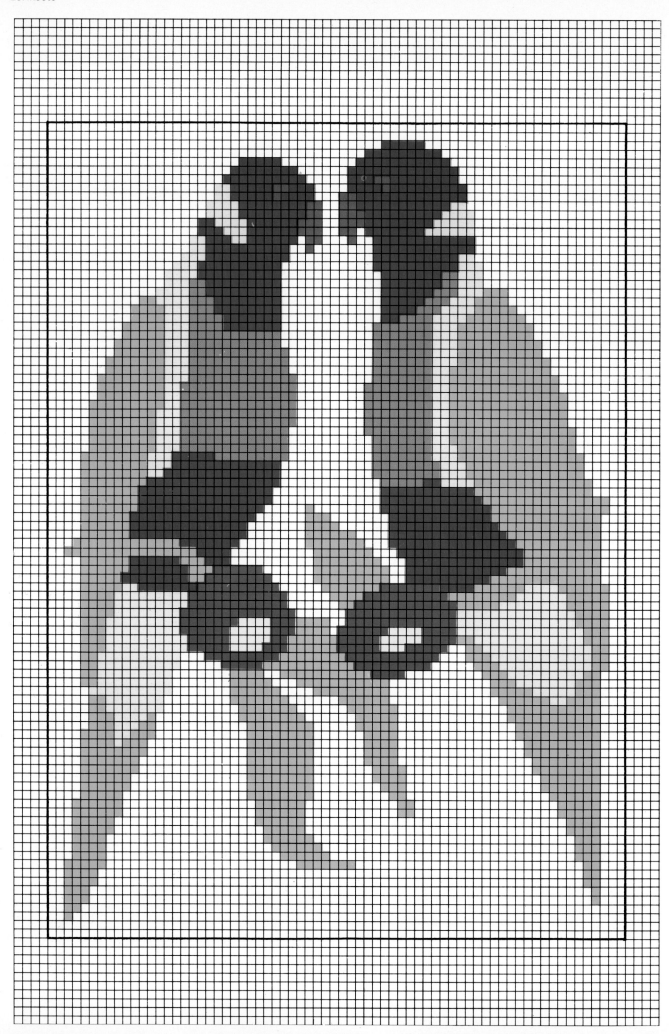

Blue (m.c.)

Yellow

Leaf green

Pink

Royal blue

Red

Green

Orange

side of hood facing, pick up 78 sts. Rib (K.1, P.1) for 4 rows. Cast off.

To make up

Sew up all raglan, side and sleeve seams with back st. Fold hems under and slip st. into position.

Neckband   Beginning at right front neck edge, with 3.75m needles and m.c., and right side facing, pick up 75 sts ending at left front edge (19 sts front, 9 sts sleeve, 19 sts back, 9 sts sleeve, 19 sts front).

1st row: P.1, (K.1, P.1) to end of row.

2nd row: K.1, (P.1, K.1) to end of row.

Repeat both rows once more. Cast off.

Right front band   Beginning at right front hem, with 3.75m needles and m.c., and right side facing, pick up 82 sts evenly, ending at neck edge.

1st row: Rib (K.1, P.1) to end.

2nd row: Rib (K.1, P.1) for 28 sts, * yfwd K.2 tog., rib 8 sts, * rep. from * to * 3 more times, yfwd K.2 tog., rib 6 sts, yfwd K.2 tog., rib 2 sts.

3rd and 4th rows: Rib (K.1, P.1) to end of row. Cast off.

Left front band   As for right front band omitting button holes. Sew on buttons to match button hole spacing. Sew on hood to bottom of neck band. Weave in loose threads.

Boomerang

The pattern for this jumper is based on the abstract design for a boomerang used by the Aboriginals to decorate shields. As an interesting alternative, the beige lines could be knitted in a contrast yarn, such as metallic silver or gold, or a heavily textured shaggy yarn.

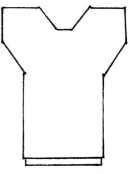

Front and back

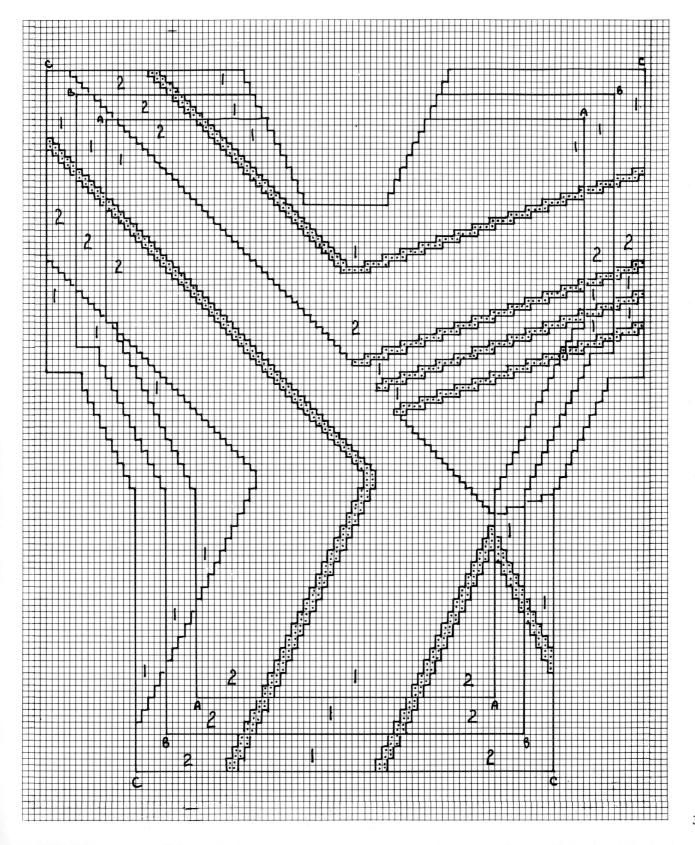

Materials
Strutt's Milford Knitting Cotton No.
4, 50 gm balls
5, 6, 6 balls brown
3, 4, 4 balls black
1 ball beige
1 pair 4.5m needles
1 pair 7.0m needles

Measurement
To fit:
A 80 cm chest/bust
B 85 cm chest/bust
C 90 cm chest/bust

Tension
13½ sts to 10 cm using two
strands of cotton and 7.0m
needles over st. st.

Note
1 Use two strands of cotton
throughout, taking one strand from
the outside and one from the inside
of the ball.
2 If preferred, one side may be
reversed in design, allowing the
design to match at one side and
shoulder seams. See explanatory
instructions in section on reversing
a graph.

☐ Brown

☐ Black

· Beige

3 Where only one figure is given,
it refers to all sizes.

Front and back
Knit two pieces in the same way
(reversing one design if preferred).
Using 4.5m needles and brown
cotton, cast on 50, 60, 70 sts. Rib
(K.1, P.1) for 10 rows. Change to
7.0m needles and work from graph
to size chosen.
Sleeve At row 35, 41, 47 inc. 1 st.
at each end of this and every alt.
row, 13, 11, 9 times. Work 1 purl
row. At beg. of next 2 rows, cast on
2, 4, 6 sts (80, 90, 100 sts).
Continue working straight for 18,
22, 26 rows.
Neck Cast off centre 14 sts, work
to end of row. Dec. 1 st. at neck
edge every knit row 6, 8, 10 times.
Work 1 row and cast off loosely 27,
30, 33 sts. Join yarn to rem. sts
and complete other side to
correspond.

To make up
Using back st. join one shoulder.
With right side facing and 4.5m
needles pick up 70, 82, 94 sts. Rib
(K.1, P.1) for 6 rows. Cast off
loosely in rib. Sew up rem. shoulder
seam and join ribbing neatly. Sew
up side seams. Work 3 rows of knit
st. crochet around armholes.
Alternatively, work 4 rows in knit
st. crochet around neckline after
sewing up both shoulder seams.
Weave in any loose threads.

Koala

The natural colours of Australian
fleece lend themselves beautifully
to animal designs.

Materials

400, 500, 600 gm natural white
(m.c.)
140 gm natural grey
40 gm natural dark brown/grey
70 gm green (white yarn dyed)
4 leather gum leaf shapes
(optional)
1 pair 6.5m needles
1 pair 8.0m needles

Note

The yarn is spun thick and thin and
in single ply. It is thicker than most
commercial yarns.

Yarn substitute

Patons Herdwick 8 ply wool 50 gm
balls
14, 16, 18 balls white
3 balls light grey
1 ball dark grey or brown
2 balls green
Use 2 strands of Herdwick
throughout.

Measurement

To fit:
A   80 cm chest/bust
B   85 cm chest/bust
C   90 cm chest/bust

Tension

12 sts to 10 cm using 8.0m needles
over st. st. and handspun yarn or 2
strands of 8 ply Herdwick.

Note

Where only one figure is given, this
applies to all sizes.

☐	White (m.c.)
K̄	Natural grey
Ḡ	Green (dyed)
X̄	Natural black
·	Armhole marker

Back

Using 6.5m needles and m.c., cast
on 42, 46, 50 sts. Rib (K.1, P.1) for
10 rows. Change to 8.0m needles
and work in st. st. At row 55 put in
coloured thread markers at each
end of row to indicate armholes.
Continue straight until 82 rows
have been worked (57, 57, 59.5
cm). Cast off centre 16 sts. Work to
end of row. Work 4 rows with no
shaping. Cast off. Join yarn to
remaining sts and work other side
to correspond.

Front

As for back till row 74, 74, 78 but
work from graph. Begin neck
shaping for all sizes at next row.
Cast off centre 8 sts. Work to end
of row. Dec. 1 st. at neck edge
every alt. row 4 times (13, 15, 17
sts remain). Work 4 rows. Cast off.
Join yarn to remaining sts and
work to correspond.

Sleeves

Using 6.5m needles and m.c., cast
on 26, 26, 30 sts. Rib (K.1, P.1) for
10 rows. Inc. 1 st. at each end of
5th row and then every 6th row
until 46, 46, 50 sts remain. Work
straight for required length. Cast
off 6 sts at beg. of next 6 rows.
Cast off 10, 10, 14 sts.

To make up

Using back st. sew up one
shoulder. With 6.5m needles and
right side facing, pick up 62 sts
evenly. Rib (K.1, P.1) for 16 rows.
Cast off very loosely in rib. Fold
neckband in half and slip st. to
inside. Using armhole markers as
guides sew in sleeves. Sew up side
and sleeve seams. Weave in loose
threads.
Cut four gum leaves out of leather
scraps, using a real gum leaf for a
pattern. With machine thread,
secure leaves in position by their
stems.

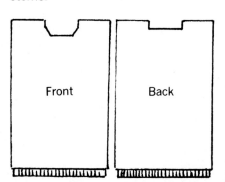

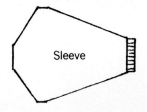

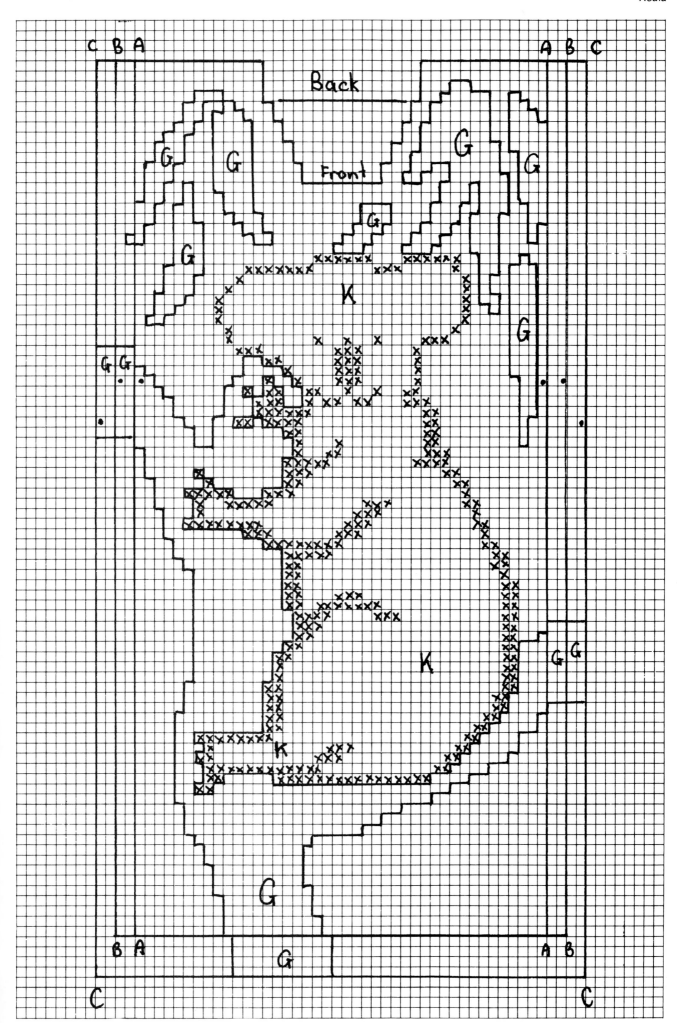

Flannel Flower

The flower wraps around the jumper with its green centre at your side. Embroider the green tips later if you wish.

Materials
Patons Family 12 ply 50 gm balls
12 balls black (m.c.)
3 balls white
1 ball grey-green
1 pair 4.5m needles
1 circular 6.0m needle, 96 cm long
1 set of 4, 4.5m needles

Measurement
Fits up to 100 cm chest/bust.

Tension
16 sts to 10 cm using 6.0m needles and Patons Jet over st. st.

Front   Back

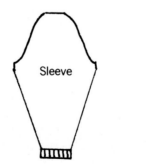

Sleeve

☐ Black (m.c.)

[w] White

[X] Grey-green

Note
Front and back knitted together until armholes. Work along rows, turning at end of each row, not working in the round. At armholes, work front first, then back separately.

Front and back
Using 4.5m needles and m.c., cast on 159 sts. Rib for 15 rows (K.2, P.2). Change to the circular needle and work from graph.
Armhole   At row 81 commence armhole shaping. Cast off 4 sts at beginning of this row, K.72 sts from graph, cast off 8 sts, K. to end of row from graph.
Next row: Cast off 4 sts at beg. of row, purl to end of row. This section is the front and should be completed first. Cast off 2 sts at beg. of next 2 rows. Work without shaping till row 111.
Neck   Cast off centre 22 sts. Dec. 1 st. at neck edge every row till 13 sts remain. Work 4 rows without shaping.
Shoulder   Cast off 6 sts at beginning of next row and 7 sts at beg. of next alt. row. Join yarn to left front and work to correspond.

Back
Join yarn ready for purl row. Cast off 2 sts at beg. of next 2 rows. Work without shaping until row 125. Cast off 6 sts at beg. of next 2 rows, then cast off 7 sts at beg. of following 2 rows, then cast off 42 sts once.

Sleeves
Using 4.5m needles and m.c., cast on 46 sts. Rib (K.2, P.2) for 10 rows. Change to 6.0m needles and work in st. st. Inc. 1 st. at each end of 5th row, then every 6th row till 70 sts. Work 7 rows straight.
Armhole   Cast off 3 sts at beg. of next 2 rows*. Then dec. 1 st. each end of next and every alt. row till 30 sts. Cast off.
Alternate sleeve   Smooth fitting with no gathers. Work as for original sleeve instruction to *. Then dec. 1 st. each end of next and every row till 22 sts remain. Cast off. Set sleeve in smoothly.

To make up
Using back st. sew up shoulder and side seams. Sew up sleeve seam. Set in sleeve, putting in tucks and gathers at shoulder.
Neckband   Using a set of 4.5m needles, pick up evenly 112 sts. Rib (K.2, P.2) for 20 rows. Cast off loosely in rib. Fold neckband in half and slip st. to inside. Weave in all loose threads.

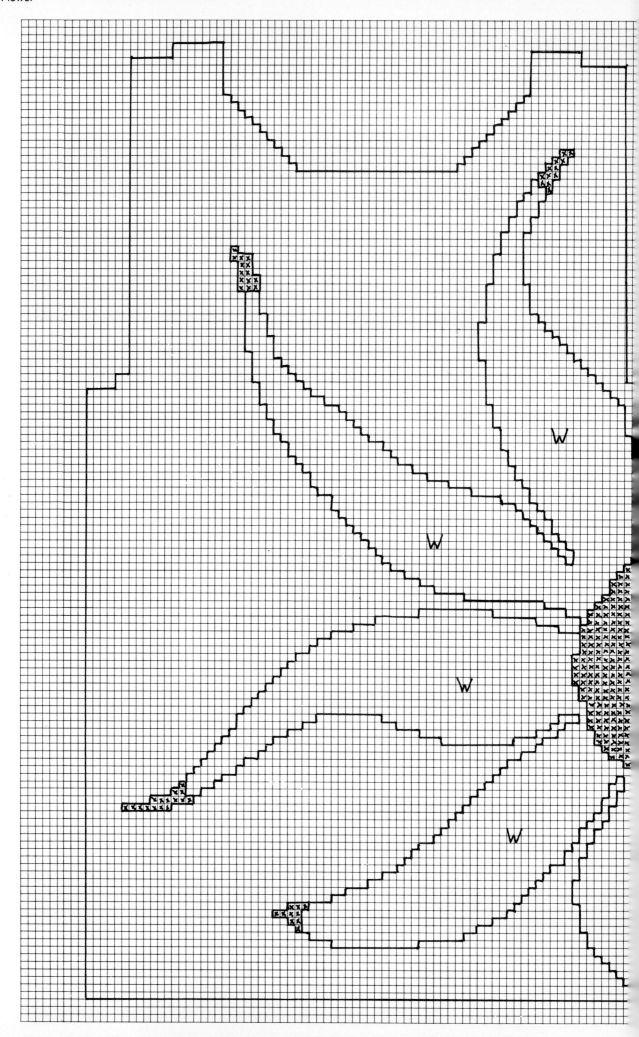

Parrots

This jumper was originally designed to use up a lot of different blues and the effect was eye-catching. However, you can use one shade of blue for the background (mid-blue, not navy blue so that the bright parrot colours will stand out).

Materials

12 ply wool 50 gm balls
2 (4) balls dark blue
2 balls mid-blue
1 ball teal blue
1 ball aqua
1 ball pale blue
2 balls blue
1 ball apple green
1 ball olive green
1 ball light green
1 ball bright red
1 ball navy blue
small quantity yellow-orange
small quantity dark red
small quantity light grey
1 pair 4.5m needles
1 pair 6.0m needles

Apple green

Olive green

Light green

Bright red

Dark red

Navy blue

Yellow-orange

Light-grey

1 Mid-blue

2 Blue

3 Teal blue

4 Aqua

5 Pale blue

6 Dark blue

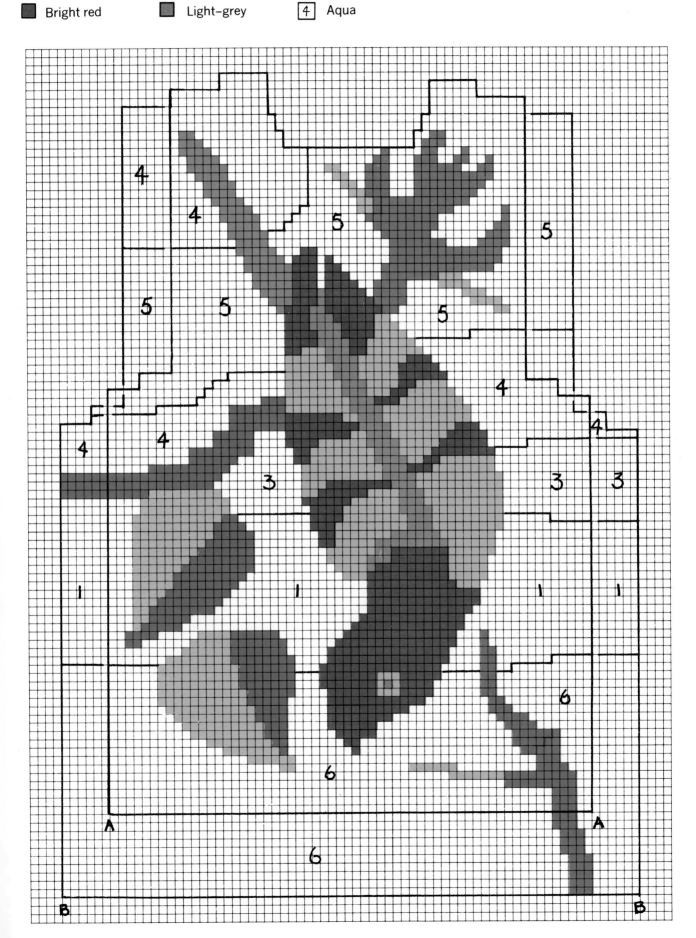

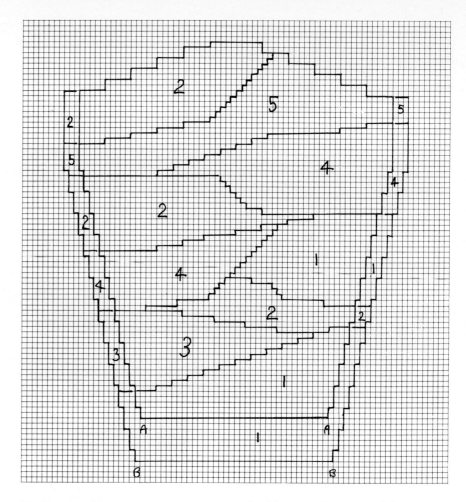

Measurement
To fit:
A   78 cm chest/bust
B   82 cm chest/bust

Tension
16 sts to 10 cm using 12 ply and
6.0m needles over st. st.

Note
Where only one figure is given, this
applies to both sizes.

Front and back
Alike. Using dark blue yarn and
4.5m needles, cast on 60, 72 sts.
Rib (K.1, P.1) for 10 rows. Change
to 6.0m needles and work from
graph.
Armholes   Begin armhole shaping
at row 51, 57. Cast off 4 sts at beg.
of next 4 rows. Continue straight
till row 81, 91.
Neck   Cast off centre 16 sts. Dec.
1 st. at neck edge for next two alt.
rows.
Shoulder   Size A: Work 2 rows
straight, then cast off 6 sts at beg.
of next 2 purl rows.
Size B: Cast off 6 sts at beg. of next
3 purl rows.
Join yarn to remaining sts and
work to correspond, reversing
instructions.

Sleeves
Using dark blue and 4.5m needles,
cast on 30, 32 sts. Rib (K.1, P.1)

for 10 rows. Change to 6.0m
needles and work from graph. Inc.
6 sts evenly along first row (36, 38
sts). Inc. 1 st. each end of 3rd row,
then every 4th row till 60, 66 sts.
Work 14 rows without shaping.
Size A: Cast off 5 sts at beg. of next
10 rows. Cast off 10 sts once.
Size B: Cast off 8 sts at beg. of next
2 rows, then 5 sts at beg. of next 8
rows, 10 sts once.

To make up
Sew up one shoulder. With mid-
blue and 4.5m needles, and right
side facing, pick up 70 sts. Rib
(K.1, P.1) for 12 rows. Cast off
loosely in rib. Sew up rem. shoulder
and join neckband. Fold neckband
in half and slip st. loosely to inside.
Sew side and sleeve seams. Set
sleeve in and sew. Weave in loose
threads. Press if required.

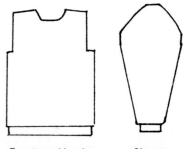

Front and back   Sleeve

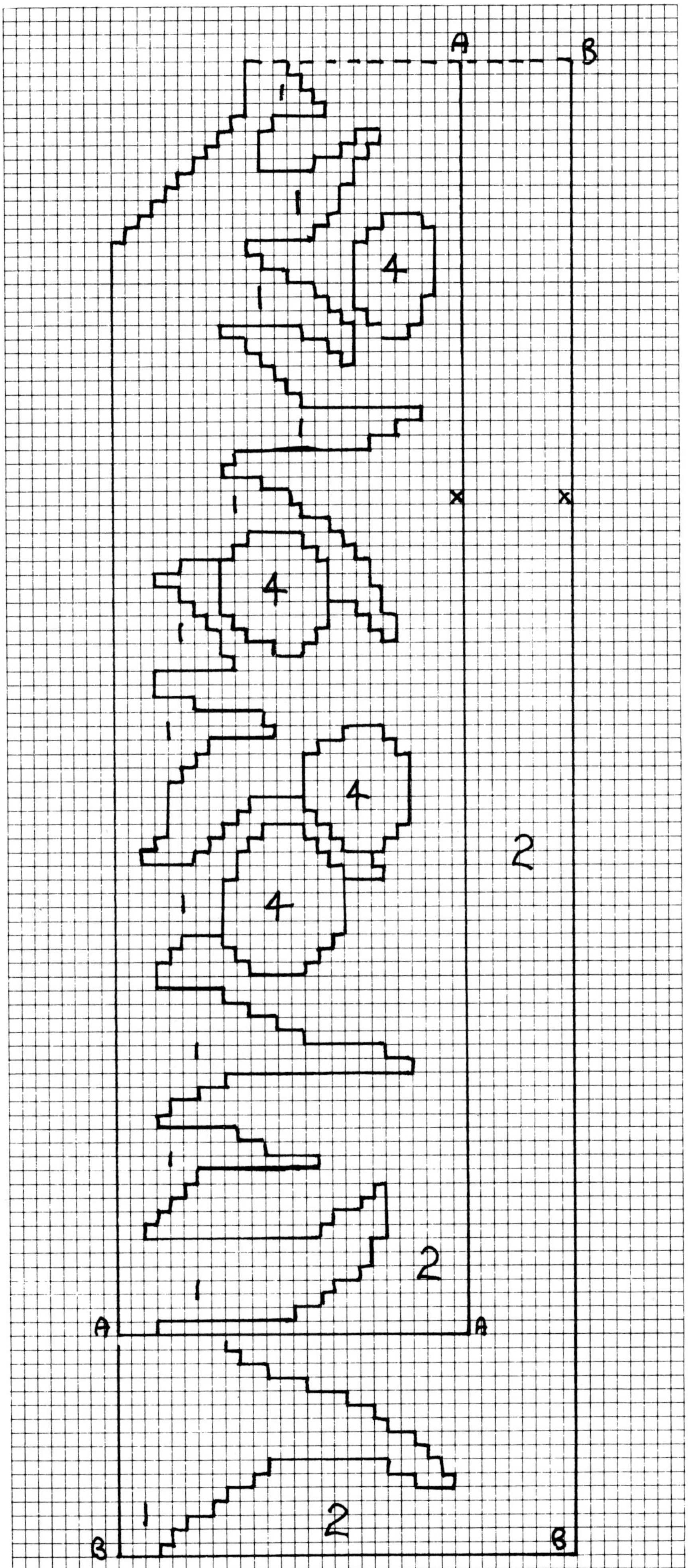

Sleeve and yoke

Possum

A different species of possum appears on each side of this jumper — the fat-tailed one is a little sugar glider and the other is a ring-tail. And as they move around at night, choose a very dark fleece for the background.

Materials
Hand-spun yarn, double ply
370, 470 gm black (m.c.)
216, 316 gm grey
94 gm yellow (vegetable-dyed)
40 gm white
1 pair 6.0m needles
1 pair 8.0m needles

Yarn substitute
Patons 8 ply Herdwick 50 gm balls
14, 16 balls dark grey or dark brown
7, 8 balls light grey
1 ball white
Patons 8 ply Totem 50 gm balls
2 balls pale yellow
Use 2 strands of Herdwick and 2 strands of Totem throughout.

Tension
12 sts to 10 cm over st. st. using handspun yarn or 2 strands of Herdwick and 8.0m needles (or whichever needles will give the correct tension).

Measurement
A   Fits up to 92 cm chest/bust. Yoke measures from wrist to wrist 134 cm and 22 cm wide from shoulder to chest.
B   Fits up to 98 cm chest/bust. Yoke measures from wrist to wrist 144 cm and 30 cm wide from shoulder to chest.

Note
1   The design can be adapted to suit a man's jumper. Sleeves usually need to be longer and some of the yellow blossoms can be omitted.
2   Where only one figure is given it refers to both sizes.

2	Black (m.c.)
1	Grey
3	White
4	Yellow

49

Sleeve and yoke

Work two pieces in the same way. Refer to detailed instructions in 'Reversing a graph' as yoke graph needs to be reversed. Using 8.0m needles and m.c., cast on 26, 34 sts and work from the graph. At row 61, 77 put in coloured thread as body marker. At row 80, 96 begin neck shaping by dec. 1 st. at neck edge of this row and following 10 rows (16, 24 sts rem.). Work 3 rows straight ending with a purl row on wrong side. This is the half-way mark. Now turn graph upside down and commence working from graph to complete other half. Next row should be a knit row. Read the graph from left to right and *not* right to left as before. Work 3 more rows straight. Next row, inc. 1 st. at neck edge till 26, 34 sts. Work straight till graph completed. Cast off.

Body

Work two pieces in the same way but follow different graphs. Using 6.0m needles and m.c., cast on 54 sts. Rib (K.1, P.1) for 10 rows. Change to 8.0m needles and work from graph. Cast off loosely.

Gussets

Make two gussets. Using 8.0m needles cast on 6 sts and work 8 rows in st. st. Cast off.

To make up

Cuff   Sew up one shoulder seam. Using 6.0m needles and m.c., with right side of wrist facing, pick up 28, 36 sts. Rib (K.1, P.1) for 16 rows. Cast off in rib.

Neckband   Using 6.0m needles and grey yarn, with right side of neck facing, pick up 56 sts. Rib (K.1, P.1) for 14 rows. Cast off very loosely in rib. Sew up rem. shoulder seam. Join neckband rib with a flat seam. Fold neckband in half and slip st. loosely to inside.

Cuff   Follow previous instructions and knit the second cuff in rib. With back st. sew body to yoke using body markers as guides. Sew up side and sleeve seams leaving seams open for gusset. Gusset is stitched in diagonally.
Weave in loose ends.

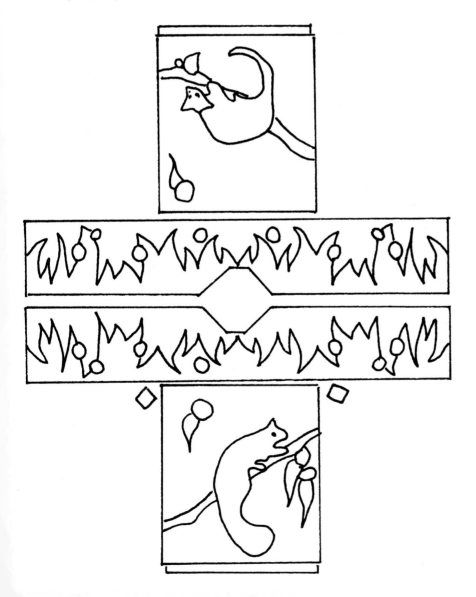

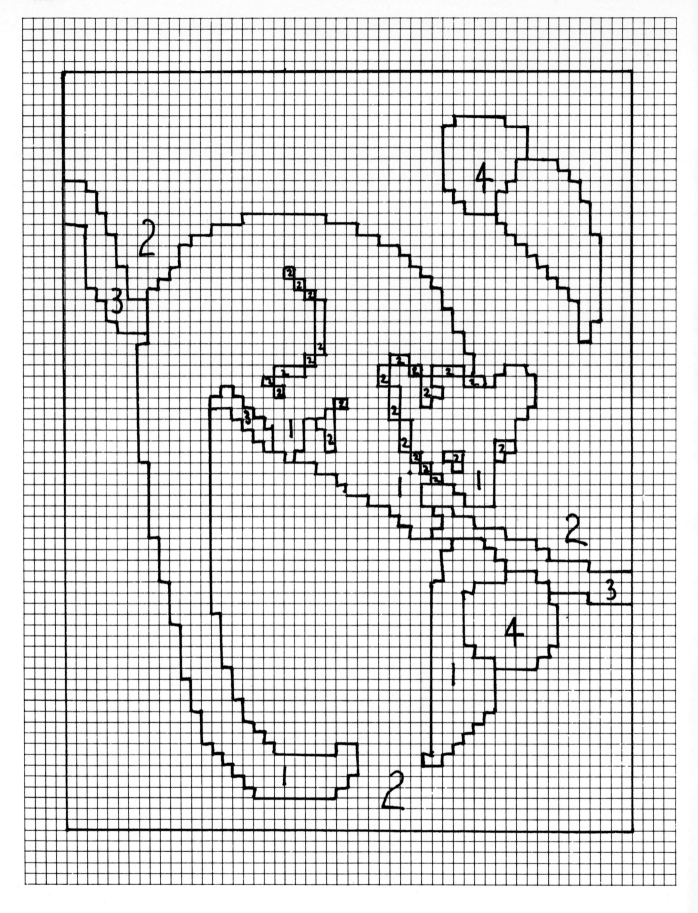

2 Black (m.c.)

1 Grey

3 White

4 Yellow

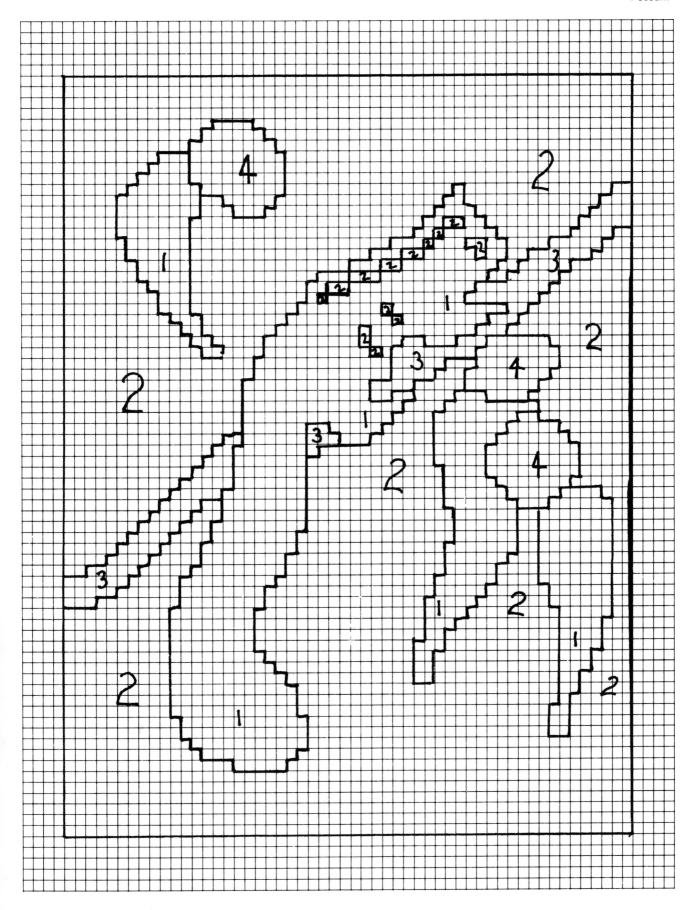

Cockatoos

An easy-to-wear jumper for men or
women with a cockatoo or corella
on the front. Change the main
colour, if you wish, to a darker or
brighter tone and the other colours
will still work well.

☐ Dusky blue (m.c.)	⊡ White	▨ Tan
☐ Lemon–yellow	▨ Pink	▨ Black
▨ Yellow–gold	▨ Grey–green	▨ Grey

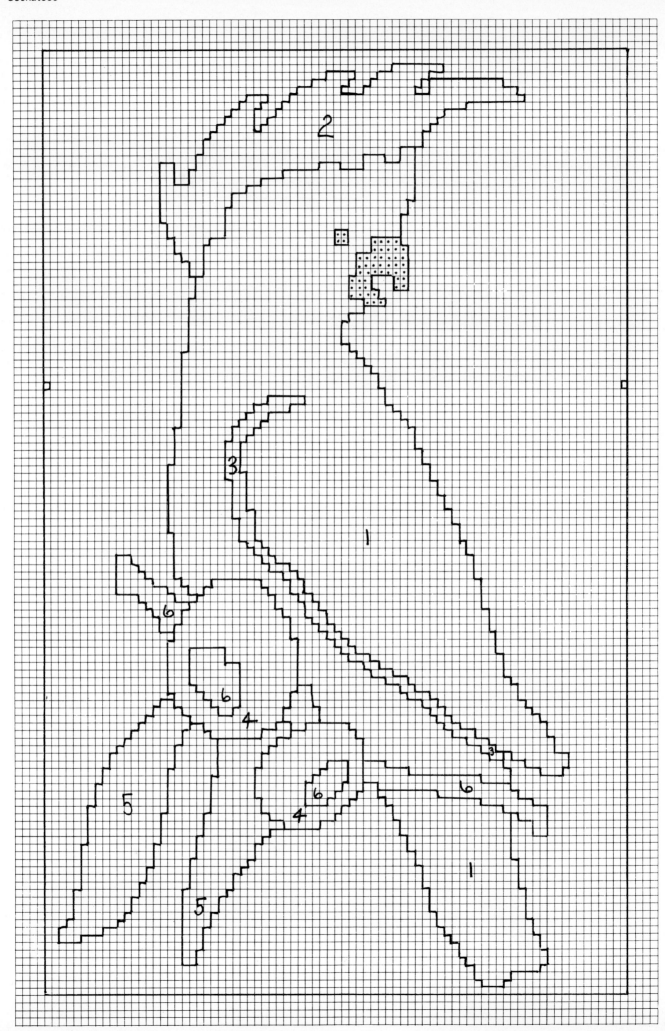

Materials
Cleckheaton 12 ply 50 gm balls
12 balls dusky blue (m.c.)
4 balls natural white
1 ball yellow
1 ball grey-green
1 ball salmon pink
1 ball lemon-yellow
small quantity tan
small quantity grey
small quantity black
1 pair 4.5m needles
1 pair 6.0m needles

Note
If some colours are hard to find, use two strands (as one strand) of an 8 ply yarn in the appropriate colour. Don't improvise in this way for the ground colour or the white bodies of the birds.

Measurement
To fit up to 98 cm chest/bust.

Tension
16 sts to 10 cm over st. st. using 6.0m needles.

☐ Dusky blue (m.c.)

1 White

2 Yellow–gold

3 Lemon–yellow

4 Pink

5 Grey–green

6 Tan

• Black

Front and back
Similar, except each has a different graph to be followed.
Using 4.5m needles and m.c., cast on 80 sts. Rib (K.1, P.1) for 10 rows. Change to 6.0m needles and work from graph.
Row 80: Put in a coloured thread to indicate armhole.
Row 126: Still using 6.0m needles, work 10 rows of rib (K.1, P.1).
Cast off very loosely in rib.

Sleeves
Using 4.5m needles and m.c. cast on 46 sts. Rib (K.1, P.1) for 10 rows. Change to 6.0m needles and work in st. st. Increase 1 st. at each end of 5th row and then every 6th row until 70 sts. Work 18 rows with no increase (30 rows for men's jumpers or to length desired). Cast off loosely.

To make up
Flat st. all rib sections. Sew up 25 rib sts as shoulder seam. With back st. sew in sleeve, stretching slightly to fit armhole markers. Back st. sleeve and side seams.

Front and back alike

Sleeve

Australia

Knitted in Australia's colours of green and gold, this jumper brings to mind the unforgettable victory of *Australia II* in the America's Cup. The yoke takes its inspiration from the spinnaker of the famous yacht and is worked in picture knitting. AUSTRALIA is worked in Fair Isle method.

☐	m.c.
1	White
2	Yellow
X	Black

GRAPH A

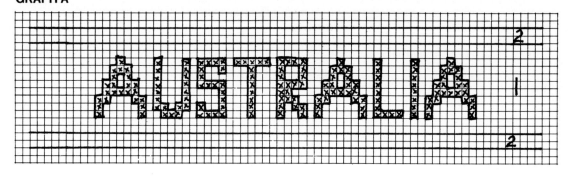

GRAPH B

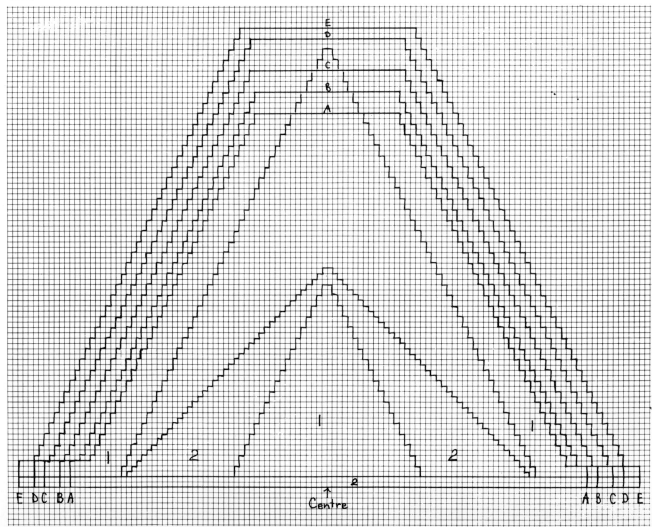

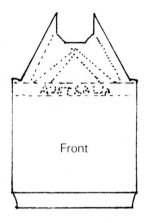

Front

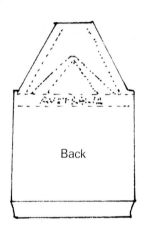

Back

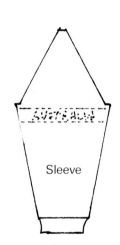

Sleeve

Materials
8 ply wool 50 gm balls
8, 9, 9, 9, 10 balls green (m.c.)
1, 1, 1, 2, 2 balls yellow
2, 3, 3, 3, 3 balls white
1 ball black
1 pair 3.25m needles
1 set 3.25m needles
1 pair 4.00m needles
1 set 4.00m needles
2 stitch holders

Measurement
To fit:
A 81 cm chest/bust
B 86 cm chest/bust
C 91 cm chest/bust
D 97 cm chest/bust
E 102 cm chest/bust

Tension
22 sts to 10 cm using 4.0m needles
(or whichever needles will give the
correct tension).

Back
With green and 3.25m needles, cast
on 90, 94, 100, 104, 110 sts. Rib
(K.1, P.1) for 6cm, inc. evenly 10 sts
along last row of rib to 100, 104,
110, 114, 120 sts.
Change to 4.0m needles and work
in stocking st. for 31, 31, 31, 32, 33
cm, ending on a P. row.
Begin the 16 rows of Graph A. Use
Fair Isle method for the letters, but
2 separate balls of white for the
spaces either side. Twist the black
and white threads of the letters
around the white yarn at either end
of the row. Place letters thus: K.24,
26, 29, 31, 34 white, K.52 of black
and white letters, K.24, 26, 29, 31,
34 white.
On completion of the 16 rows, work
Graph B thus: K.10, 12, 15, 17, 20
white, K.1 green, K.21 yellow, K.36
white, K.21 yellow, K.1 green, K.10,
12,15, 17, 20 white (7 separate
balls of yarn). Work pattern in
picture knitting method, twisting
colours at colour changes.
At the same time, begin armhole
shaping on 3rd row of large pattern.
Cast off 4, 4, 4, 3, 3 sts at beg. of
next 2 rows. Dec. 1 st. at each end
of every knit row thus: K.2, sl. 1,
K.1, psso, K. to last 4 sts, K.2 tog,
K.2. 2nd and all alternate rows: P.
across in correct colours. Dec. in
this manner until 28, 28, 30, 30, 34
sts remain. Slip sts onto holder.

Front
As for back until 56, 56, 58, 58, 62
sts remain of reglan shaping,
ending on a P. row.
Shape neck: Keep pattern and
raglan dec. in order, K.21, 21, 22,
21, 22 sts, turn. Dec. 1 st. at neck
edge every row until 11, 11, 10, 11
sts remain. Keep neck edge straight
and cont. raglan, dec. until 3 sts.
K.1, sl. 1, psso.
Next row: P.2, turn, K.2 tog., fasten
off. Slip next 12, 12, 12, 14, 16 sts
onto holder.
Complete other side to correspond,
working K.2 tog. in place of sl. 1,
K.1, psso.

Sleeves
With green and 3.25m needles, cast
on 48, 48, 50, 50, 52 sts. Rib (K.1,
P.1) for 6cm, and inc. 4 sts evenly
along last row of rib to 52, 52, 54,
54, 56 sts.
Change to 4.0m needles and work
in stocking st. Inc. 1 st. at each end
of 5th and then every 6th row until
78, 82, 84, 88, 94 sts.
At the same time, when sleeve edge
measures 37, 37, 37, 38, 42 cm,
begin the 16 rows of Graph A.
Position letters thus: using same
method as for back: K.13, 15, 16,
18, 21 white, K.52 black and white
letters, K.13, 15, 16, 18, 21 white.
On completion of graph work 2 rows
of green and begin raglan shaping
as for back. When 6, 6, 4, 4, 6 sts
remain, work 1 row P. and cast off.
Work other sleeve to correspond.

Make up
Press.
Neckband: Join raglan seams. With
a set of 3.25m needles and green,
and with right side facing, begin at
left back sleeve seam and knit up
100, 100, 106, 106, 110 sts evenly
including stitches from holders. Rib
(K.1, P.1) for 6 cm and cast off very
loosely in rib.
Polo collar: Work neckband as
above, but after 6 cm change to a
set of 4.0m needles and rib until
collar measures 16 cm. Cast off
loosely in rib.
Back stitch side and sleeve seams,
flat sew rib. Fold crew neck in half
to inside and slip stitch into place.
Tidy up threads by weaving in with
a crochet hook.

Snake

Another aboriginal design. Retain the earthy ochre tones, but the white outlines could be done in textured yarn. Or perhaps change the black to a shiny black yarn. If you feel like a challenge, knit the snake with black sequins threaded on to the black yarn.

☐ Olive (m.c.)

1 White

2 Black

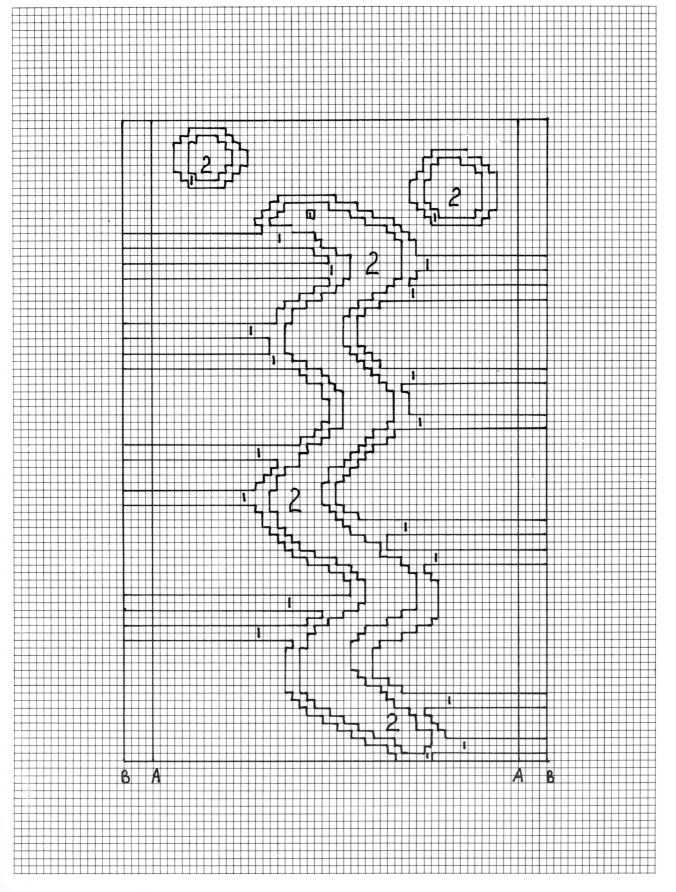

Materials

Strutt's Milford Knitting Cotton
No.4, 50 gm balls
6, 7 balls olive (m.c.) (No. 93)
2 balls black
3 balls white
1 pair 5.5m needles
1 pair 7.0m needles

Measurement

To fit:
A   80–85 cm chest/bust
B   90–95 cm chest/bust

Tension

13½ sts to 10 cm, using two
strands of yarn and 7.0m needles
over st. st.

Note

1   Use two strands of cotton
throughout, taking one strand from
the outside and the other from the
inside of the ball.
2   Where only one figure appears,
it refers to both sizes.

Front and back

Both pieces are exactly alike. Using
5.5m needles and m.c., cast on 50,
58 sts. Rib (K.1, P.1) for 10 rows.
Change to 7.0m needles and work
from graph. At row 65, put in
coloured thread markers for
armholes. On completion of graph,
change to white cotton. Retaining
7.0m needles, rib (K.1, P.1) 10
rows. Cast off very loosely in rib.

To make up

Sew 10 cm along both shoulders,
using a flat seam. With 5.5m
needles and right side facing, pick
up 58 sts, beginning and ending at
an armhole marker. Rib (K.1, P.1)
for 5 rows. Cast off loosely in rib.
Join armhole ribbing. Sew up side
seams. Weave loose threads into
work.

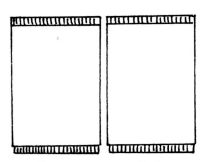

Front   Back

Wattle
Twinset

The versatile wattle lends itself to a
design for a twinset. This time the
wattle is a three dimensional
blossom.

Materials

Patons Gem 50 gm balls
10, 12 balls blue (m.c.)
3 balls green
1 ball yellow
8 small green buttons
6 m shirring elastic
1 4.5m circular needle
1 pair 4.5m needles
1 pair 6.5m needles
1 stitch holder

Measurement

To fit:
A   80–86 cm bust
B   86–92 cm bust

Tension

16 sts to 10 cm with 6.5m needles
and two strands of yarn over st. st.

Note

1   Use two strands of cotton
throughout, taking one strand from
the outside and one strand from
the inside of the ball.
2   Where there is only one figure,
this applies to both sizes.

Bobble

As for instructions in Billabong.

STRAPLESS TOP

Top is knitted in one piece with a
centre back seam. Using 4.5m
needles and m.c., cast on 111, 119
sts. Work 10 rows of rib (K.1, P.1).
Change to 6.5m needles and work
18 rows in st. st. Begin working
from graph on row 19: K.55, 59
m.c., K.1 green, K.55, 59 m.c. This
is the first row of graph design.
Continue this way till row 30. Begin
back shaping at row 31. Cast off
12, 16 sts at beg. of next 2 rows.
Cast off 4 sts at beg. of next 8
rows. Graph pattern should now be
completed. Keep rem. 55 sts on
holder.
Using 4.5m needles and green
yarn, with right side facing, pick up
33, 37 sts from the back, 55 sts
from holder, 33, 37 sts along other
side (121, 129 sts). Rib (K.1, P.1)
for 8 rows. Cast off very loosely in
rib.

To make up

Using back stitch, sew up centre
back. Cut 4 lengths of shirring
elastic 66, 68 cm long. Thread
through the wrong side of the top
rib. Secure with knot, and using
sewing thread stitch down. Cut 3
lengths of shirring elastic 64, 66
cm long. Thread through the wrong
side of rib at waist, using same
method as for top.

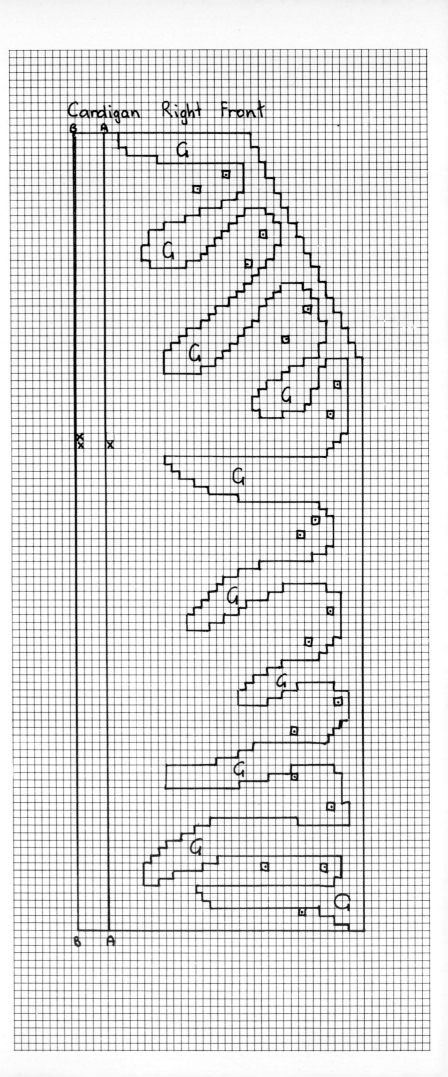

Cardigan Right Front

Blue (m.c.)

G Green

· Yellow bobble

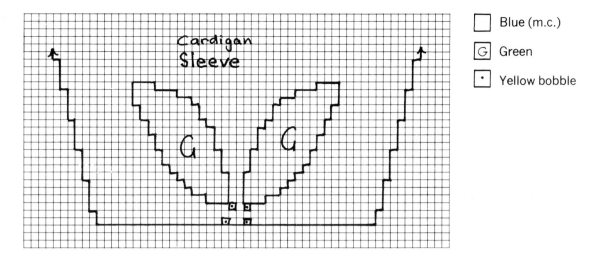

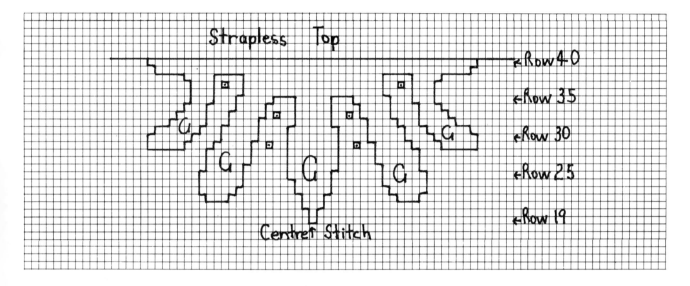

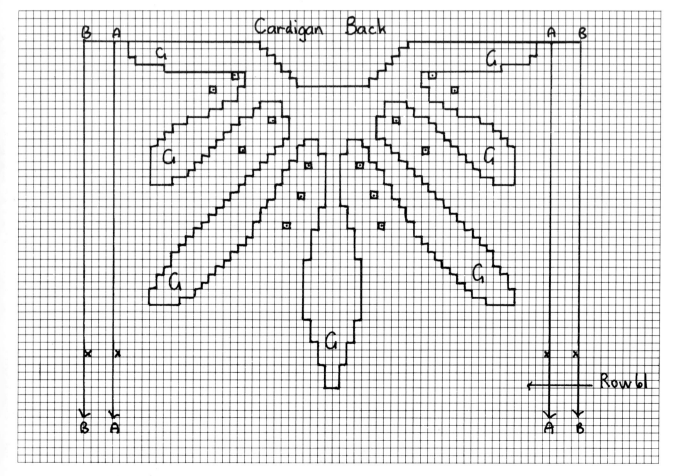

CARDIGAN

Back

Using 4.5m needles and m.c., cast on 60, 68 sts. Rib (K.1, P.1) for 12 rows. Change to 6.5m needles and work 60 rows in st. st. At row 61 commence working from graph: K.29, 33 m.c., K.2 green, K.29, 33 m.c. Put in coloured thread markers as armhole guides at row 65.

Neck shaping   At row 101, cast off centre 10 sts, work to end of row. Dec. 1 st. at neck edge for next 5 rows. Cast off final 20, 24 sts. Join to rem. sts and complete to correspond.

Right front

Using 4.5m needles and m.c., cast on 35, 39 sts. Rib (K.1, P.1) for 12 rows. Change to 6.5m needles and work from graph. At row 65 put in coloured thread markers as armhole guides. At row 75 begin V-neck shaping. Dec. 1 st. at neck edge every alt. row 15 times. Cast off final 20, 24 sts.

Left front

As for right front, but reverse the design. Refer to detailed instructions in section on 'Reversing a graph'. Read knit row from left to right instead of the traditional right to left.

Sleeves

Both sizes: Using 4.5m needles and m.c., cast on 34 sts. Rib (K.1, P.1) for 12 rows. Inc. 4 sts on last row (38 sts). Change to 6.5m needles and work from graph. Inc. 1 st. at each end of 3rd row and then every 4th row until 68 sts. Work 2 rows straight (or length required). Cast off 6 sts at beg. of next 8 rows and 20 sts once.

To make up

Sew up shoulder seams, matching designs. Sew in sleeves, using armhole markers as guides. Sew up all side and sleeve seams. With 4.5m circular needle and right side facing, pick up 75 sts beg. at right-hand front basque, 24 sts along back and 75 sts down left front (174 sts). Rib (K.1, P.1) 1 row.

Buttonholes

Row 2: K.1, P.1, K.2 tog., *(K.1, P.1) 3 times, K.2 tog.* Rep. from * to * 7 times (8 holes altogether). Continue row in rib.
Row 3: P.1, (K.1, P.1) till buttonhole reached. *Knit into front and back of next st., (K.1, P.1) 3 times*. Repeat from * to * 7 times, K.1, P.1.
Rib 3 more rows. Cast off.
Sew on buttons to correspond to holes.
Weave in loose threads. If necessary, sew bobble threads with sewing cotton to ensure that they do not show through to right side.

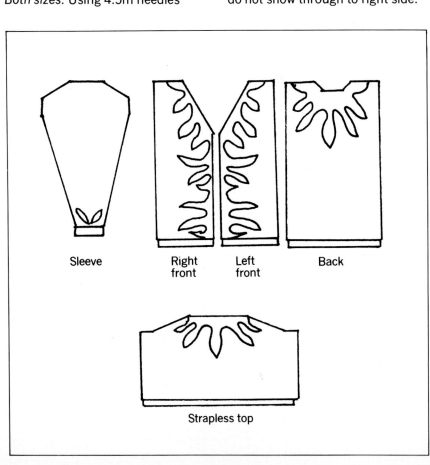

Sleeve   Right front   Left front   Back

Strapless top

Rosella

The soft textured cotton yarn helps to make this simple top easy to knit and easy to wear.

Materials
Patons Cotton Top 50 gm balls
3, 4, 4 balls natural or white
1 ball red
1 ball mid-blue
To be dyed, following directions on dye tin:
1, 1, 2 balls olive green
1 ball black
(Unwind balls into hanks for easy dyeing.)
                    or
1, 1, 2 balls leaf green
1 ball navy blue

Measurement
To fit:
A   80 cm chest/bust
B   85 cm chest/bust
C   90 cm chest/bust

Tension
14½ sts to 10 cm using one strand of Cotton Top and 6.0m needles.

Note
Where there is only one figure, this applies to all sizes.

Front
Using 4.0m needles and m.c., cast on 55, 69, 83 sts. Rib (K.1, P.1) for 10 rows. Change to 6.0m needles and work from graph. At row 55, 61, 67 put in coloured thread markers at both ends of row to mark armholes. At row 86, 96, 106 change to 4.0m needles and olive

Front   Back

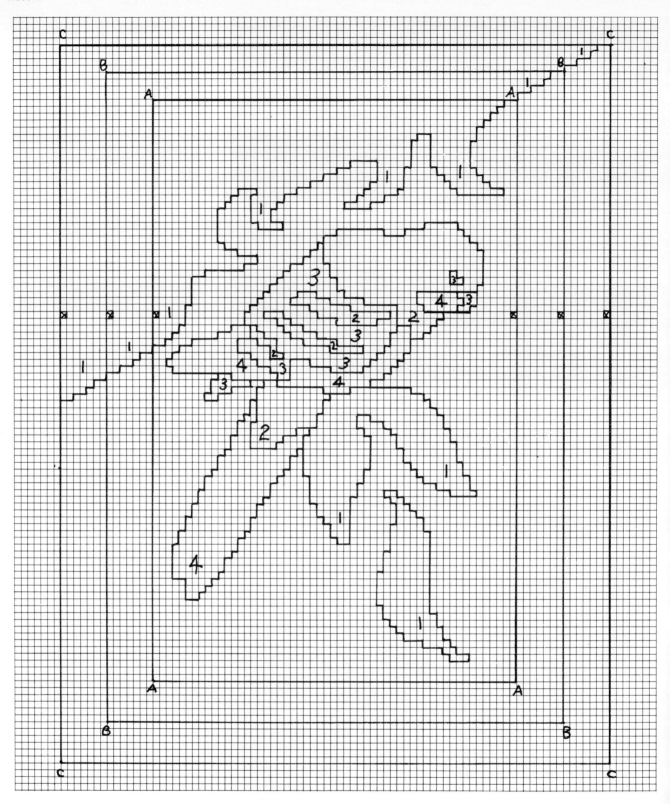

□	Natural (m.c.)
[1]	Olive green
[2]	Red
[3]	Black
[4]	Blue

green yarn and work in rib (K.1, P.1) for 10 rows.
Cast off very loosely in rib.

Back
As for front, but omit bird pattern with three leaves and work diagonal leaf pattern only. This graph needs to be reversed so that underarm and shoulder patterns will match. (Refer to section explaining graph reversal.) Commence graph with a knit row but read from left to right. At row 50, 56, 62 commence leaf pattern.

Pattern will start on a purl row read from right to left. Complete as for front.

To make up
Using a flat seam, stitch ribbing to form shoulder seams, joining 10, 17, 24 sts. Sew up side seam to underarm marks, taking care to change colour of sewing yarn. If necessary, crochet 2 rows of knit st. around armholes, one armhole in green and the other in white. Weave in loose threads.

Galah

This jumper is reversible, so either galah can be worn on the front.

Materials

Cleckheaton 12 ply wool 50 gm balls
7 balls mid-blue (m.c.)
3 balls light grey
1 ball black
1 ball light pink
1 ball mid-pink
1 ball dusky pink
2 balls bright pink
1 ball tan
2 balls green
1 pair 5.5m needles
1 pair 7.5m needles

Note

If some colours are hard to match, use two strands (as one strand) of an 8 ply wool. Do not do this for the main colour.

Measurement

To fit up to 92 cm chest/bust.

Tension

12½ sts to 10 cm using 7.5m needles and Patons Jet over st. st. This is a looser tension than usual for a standard 12 ply yarn.

Note

To match some of the colours, especially the pinks, it may be necessary to use two strands of an 8 ply yarn or choose another brand of triple knitting yarn.

Front and back

Alike. Using 5.5m needles and m.c. cast on 60 sts. Rib (K.1, P.1) for 10 rows. Change to 7.5m needles and work from graph for 28 rows. Begin dolman shaping. Inc. 1 st. at each end of every alt. row 7 times. Next knit row begin sleeve shaping. Cast on 13 sts at beg. of next 2 rows, then 10 sts at beg. of next 6 rows. Continue without shaping until row 83.

Neck   Cast off centre 14 sts. Dec. 1 st. at neck edge for next 3 rows. Work 2 rows without shaping.

Shoulder   Cast off 30 sts at beg. of next purl row, then 10 sts at beg. of next 4 purl rows, keeping neck edge straight.

Join yarn to rem. sts. Work to correspond. Shoulder shaping now occurs on knit rows.

To make up

Sew up one shoulder taking care to match designs. With 5.5m needles and m.c., and right side facing, pick up 72 sts. Rib (K.1, P.1) for 10 rows. Cast off loosely in rib. Sew up rem. shoulder and join neckband ribbing. Fold neckband in half and slip st. loosely to inside.

Cuffs   With 5.5m needles and m.c., and right side facing, pick up 38 sts. Rib (K.1, P.1) for 10 rows. Cast off loosely in rib. Sew up side seams, using flat st. for rib and back st. for seams. Weave in loose threads. Press if required.

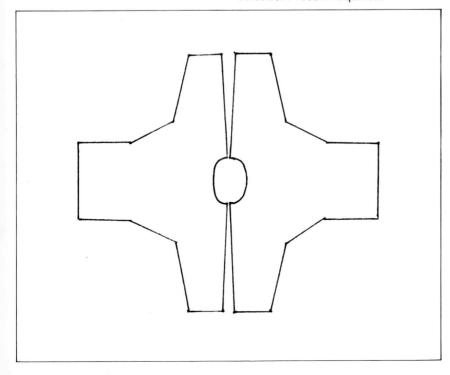

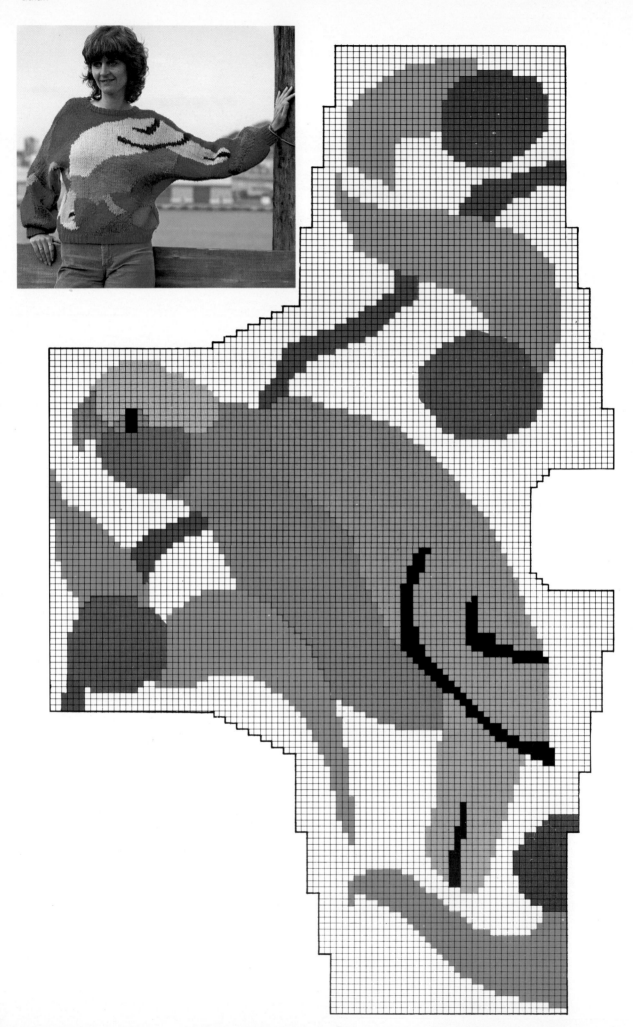

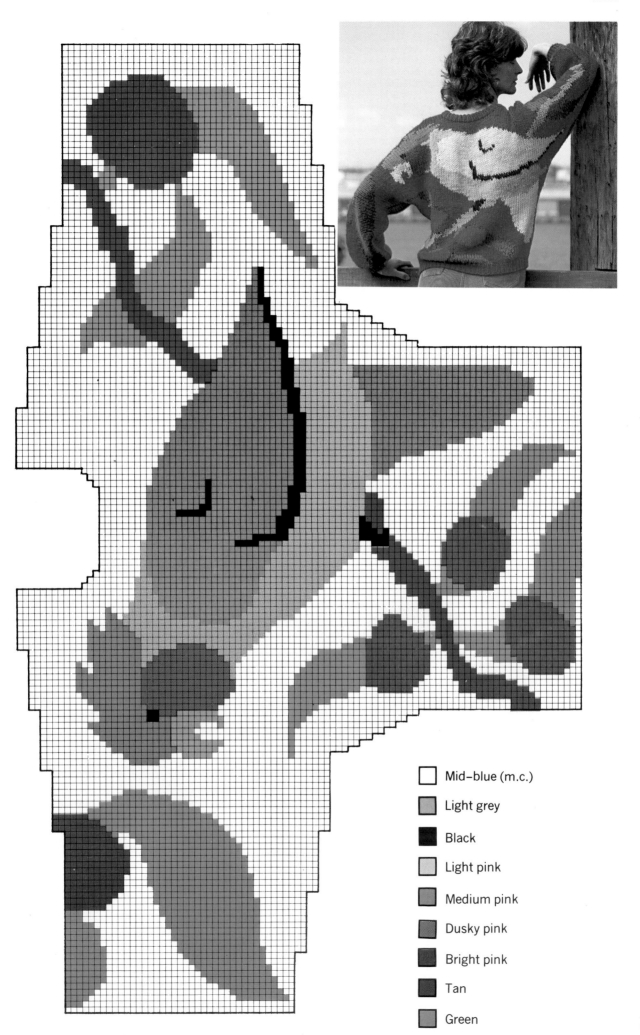

Mid–blue (m.c.)

Light grey

Black

Light pink

Medium pink

Dusky pink

Bright pink

Tan

Green

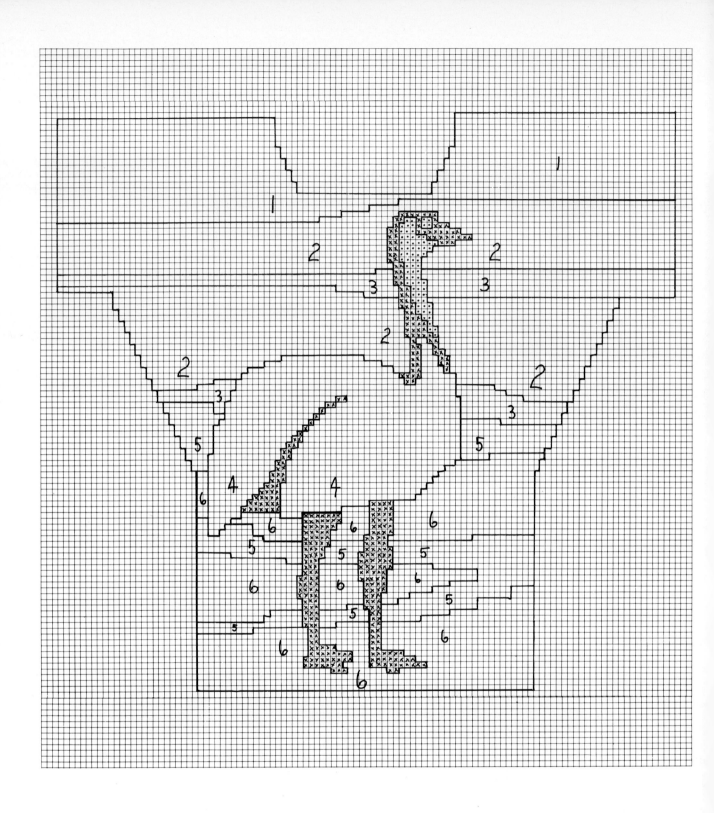

Kangaroo and Emu

Two jumpers for the effort of knitting one. Wear a different design on the front each time.

Measurement

To fit up to 95 cm bust.

Materials

Strutt's Milford Knitting Cotton No.4, 50 gm balls

or

Coton-Quik No.4, 50 gm balls

3 balls aqua

3 balls pale blue

1 ball mauve

1 ball tan

2 balls green

2 balls beige

1 ball brown

small quantity of dark blue

1 pair 5.0m needles

1 pair 7.0m needles

14.0m crochet hook

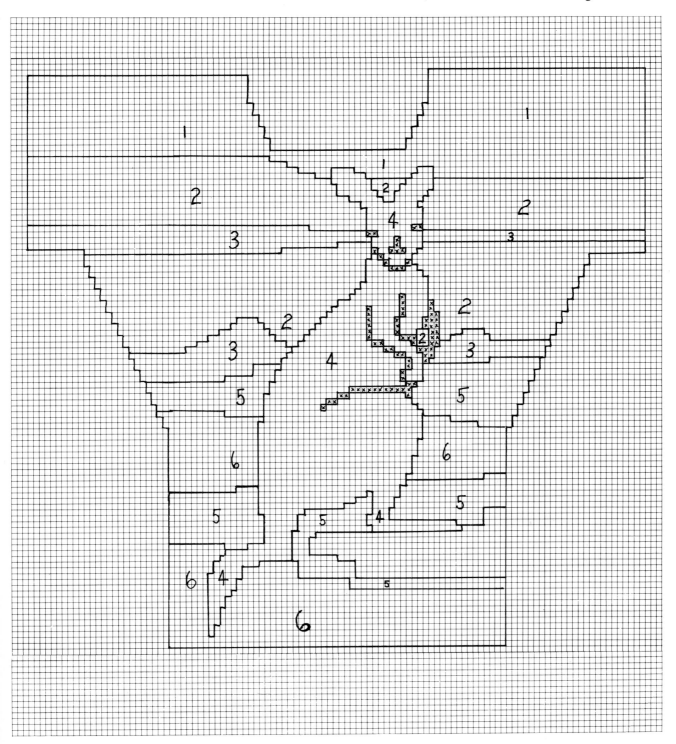

Tension

13½ sts to 10 cm using two
strands of cotton and 7.0m
needles over st. st.

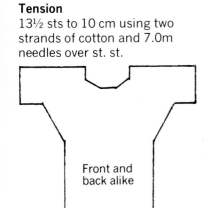

Front and
back alike

☐	Aqua
②	Light blue
③	Mauve
④	Beige
⑤	Tan
⑥	Green
X	Dark brown
·	Dark blue

Note

Use two strands of yarn throughout, taking one strand from the outside and one strand from the inside of ball.

Front and back

Two pieces are alike but follow two different graphs. Using 5.0m needles and green, cast on 60 sts. Rib (K.1, P.1) for 10 rows. Change to 7.0m needles and work from graph. At row 39 begin sleeve shaping. Inc. 1 st. at each end of this and every alt. row 15 times (90 sts). Cast on 10 sts at beg. of next 2 rows. Continue straight till neck shaping begins at row 87. Cast off centre 24 sts and dec. 1 st. at neck edge each alt. row 4 times (39 sts).

Work 4 rows straight for right shoulder. (For left shoulder work 5 rows.) Cast off. Join yarn to rem. sts and work to correspond.

To make up

Using back st., join shoulder and side seams.
With 4.0m crochet hook and 2 strands of aqua yarn, work 4 rows in knit st. crochet around neck and sleeves.
Weave in loose threads.

An important beast that has
become another symbol of
Australia. This top is easy to
convert to a dress or a man's
T-shirt. Change the background
colour if you wish, but it should be
a medium dark tone.

75

Merino

Materials
Strutt's Milford Knitting Cotton No. 4, 50 gm balls
4, 5 balls rust
1 ball black
1 ball beige
Patons Cotton Top 50 gm ball
1 ball natural
1 pair 5.5m needles
1 pair 7.0m needles
1 4.0m crochet hook

Measurement
To fit:
A 80–85 cm chest/bust
B 90–95 cm chest/bust

Tension
13½ sts to 10 cm using two strands of cotton and 7.0m needles over st. st.

Note
1 Use two strands of yarn throughout, taking one strand from the outside and one strand from the inside of each ball. Do this with the Cotton Top yarn as well.
2 Where only one figure is given, it refers to both sizes.

☐ Rust (m.c.)

⦁ Black

| I | Beige

| 2 | Natural (Cottontop)

Back
Using 5.5m needles and m.c., cast on 55, 63 sts. Rib (K.1, P.1) for 10 rows. Change to 7.0m needles and work in st. st. for 48, 54 rows.
Size A only: Shape armholes by dec. 1 st. each end of next and every alt. row 7 times.
Size B only: Shape armholes by casting off 2 sts at beg. of next 2 rows. Then dec. 1 st. each end of next and every alt. row 9 times.
Both sizes: Work 1 purl row, then commence neck shaping on following row. Cast off centre 13 sts. Work to end of row. Dec. 1 st. at neck edge for following 7 rows until 7 sts remain. Work straight for another 13 rows or length required. Cast off. Join yarn to rem. sts and work other side to correspond.

Front
As for back, but work from graph.

To make up
Use flat st. to sew up rib sections. With a back stitch sew up side and shoulder seams. Crochet 3 rounds of knit st. around neck and armholes. Weave in loose threads.

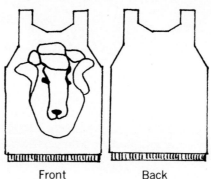

Front   Back

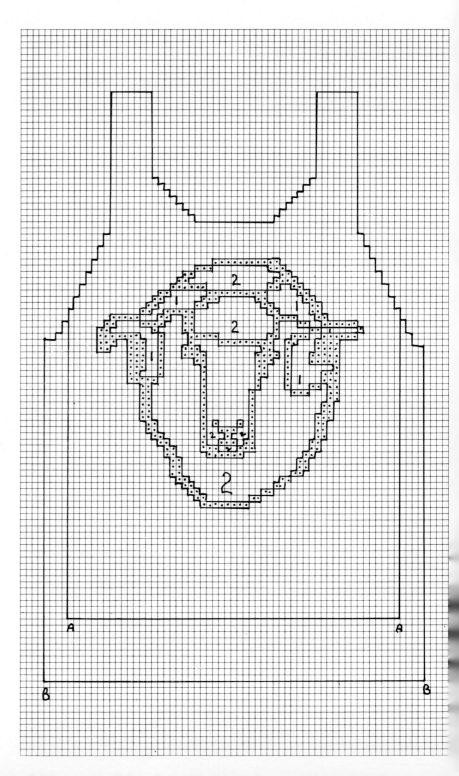

Kookaburra

Sky blue would also suit as a
background colour for the
kookaburra. Why not adapt the
design to a man's summer T-shirt?

	Olive green (m.c.)	3	Black
1	Brown	4	Beige
2	Blue	5	Rust

Materials

Strutt's Milford Knitting Cotton
No. 4, 50 gm balls
6, 7 balls olive green (m.c.)
1 ball beige
1 ball rust
1 ball brown
1 ball blue
1 ball black
1 pair 5.5m needles
1 pair 8.0m needles
1 4.0m crochet hook

Measurement

To fit:
A   80–85 cm chest/bust
B   90–95 cm chest/bust

Tension

14 sts over 10 cm using 8.0m
needles and two strands of cotton
over st. st.

Note

1   Use two strands of cotton
throughout, taking one strand from
the outside of the ball and the
other from the inside.

2   Where only one figure is given,
this refers to both sizes.

Back

Using 5.5m needles and m.c., cast
on 56, 62 sts. Rib (K.1, P.1) for 10
rows. Change to 8.0m needles and
work in st. st. for 60, 54 rows.
Begin armhole shaping by dec. 1
st. each end of next and every alt.
row 10, 13 times. At the same time
begin neck shaping on same row
as second last decrease, i.e. 9th,
11th armhole decrease. Cast off
centre 10 sts and work to end. Dec.
1 st. at neck edge for following 8
rows, keeping armhole edge
straight. Continue on these 5 sts
for 4 rows or length required. Cast
off. Join thread to remaining sts
and complete other side to
correspond.

Front

As for back but work from graph.

To make up

Flat sew rib sections, back st. side
and shoulder seams. Using 4.0m
crochet hook and 2 strands of m.c.,
knit st. crochet 2 rows around neck
edge and armholes. Weave in loose
threads.

Front   Back

Yarns

Don't skimp on quality. Pure wool yarns will knit better and keep their texture and shape better.

Experiment with brands and types of wool and yarns. A simple design can be highlighted by using a contrast textured yarn.

The important rule is to knit the background (main colour) in the one type of wool. This is also the wool to use for your sample swatch. From the sample you will determine which sized needles to use, tension, number of stitches, etc., so the main colour should occupy a large part of the design.

However, for small sections, other yarns and brands can be used very successfully, without affecting the size and shape of the jumper. So keep in mind mohair for fur, wattle, etc.; boucle for bark, pebbly ground, animals; ribbon for flowers, leaves; lurex for stars, clouds, etc.

Sometimes it may be necessary to use two or three strands of smaller ply yarn because the colour is not available in the specific ply you need. To obtain the right colour, I have used two strands of 8 ply, and even tapestry wools on occasion. Used in small sections, they have no appreciable effect on the size and shape of the jumper.

Wooden or glass beads, sequins, leather shapes and other ornaments may be threaded on to the wool before you knit with it. They can, of course, be sewn on later, but it is a much simpler operation to knit them into the garment.

Estimating yarn for jumpers

Determining how much yarn is needed for a jumper you have designed need not be difficult. Here are some steps to guide the way:

1   Compare the style of your jumper with a similar style in a knitting book. Make sure it is the same size and ply and preferably all one colour. The quantity of yarn stated is how much you need to buy. To be on the safe side, add a couple of balls to the total number. The total includes the main colour and all other colours.

2   Now determine which colour, apart from the main colour, takes up the greatest area on your jumper and estimate how many balls would be needed. Subtract this from the total number of balls.

3   Do the same for the next dominant colour, and so on. You'll probably find that most colour areas involve small quantities of yarn. These still need to be bought as one complete ball, but should not be considered as a complete ball when subtracting from the total. You can consider small colour areas in terms of half or quarter balls of yarn. Tally all these up and subtract this number from the total.

4   The result is the number you will need for the main colour.

5   Estimating quantities for novel yarns where no instructions are available, e.g. ribbon, hand-spun, strands of metallic, etc., is guess-work. But if you are prepared to knit a sample using the main colour, you will know the area knitted with one complete ball of yarn (or 100 grams in the case of hand-spun yarns). This will help in determining the total number for a one-colour jumper. Follow the other steps for other colours in your design.

6   Underestimating quantities can be very frustrating especially if it is the main colour. Other colours can be imperfectly matched or even substituted with another shade. Difficulty arises when it is impossible to obtain more of the main colour from the same dye lot. Different dye lots can produce

very different shades of the same colour. If this problem occurs, the best solution is to unpick the work to obtain at least one ball of the original main colour. Then knit in alternating pairs of rows, i.e. two rows (knit and purl) of original dye lot and two rows (knit and purl) of second dye lot. Twist threads along the edge as you take the yarn up two rows. This method will create a subtle stripe which will not be as noticeable as a solid area of a new shade.

Dyeing yarns

Many beautiful and subtle colours can be obtained from vegetable dyeing of hand-spun yarns. There are several books available which give the exact information. Two books which I have found excellent are *Dyemaking with Eucalypts* by Jean K. Carman (Rigby, 1978) and *Dyemaking with Australian Flora* prepared by the Handweavers and Spinners Guild of Victoria (Rigby, 1974). However, I have included some detailed information in the following section.

Wools and cottons can, of course, be dyed with commercial dyes, such as Dylon. Whether using vegetable or chemical dye, the yarns must be thoroughly washed, wound into hanks and tied loosely in at least two places. This allows the dye to penetrate more evenly and hastens drying. After dyeing, rinsing and drying in hanks, the yarn is wound into balls for easier handling when knitting.

With commercial dyes, follow manufacturers' instructions. Colours will be vibrant on cottons, more subtle on wool. There are many books available on chemical dyeing of yarns. Consult your local library.

Hand-spun yarn

Australia is famous for its high quality fleece. A large variety of types and colours is readily available at handcraft outlets. Spinning fleece into yarn is an age-old skill that shows no sign of disappearing. Spinning has its rewards: it is a quiet, peaceful occupation that produces spools of your own yarn. And it does not take long to spin sufficient yarn for a jumper.

There are various types of spinning wheels. A craft supplier would be able to advise on the different types and accessories. I have an Indian Head spinner which is like a large flyer unit attached to the bottom half of a treadle sewing machine table. This spinner is capable of spinning fine fleece and silk, as well as bulky yarns. When I had to use a traditional spinning wheel, I found no problem with the changeover. The spinning wheel is a simple and ancient device based on simple working principles.

CHOOSING FLEECE

A beginner in spinning should choose a Border Leicester fleece. It is a coarser wool compared with a pure Merino fleece. Merino fleece is not one to be spun in a hurry. Softness and firmness are its outstanding characteristics, and to make full use of its potential, careful handling and preparation are needed.

A good Border Leicester fleece can be spun without any preparation other than separating the locks by hand. With experience it can be spun very finely, but it also spins very easily into a soft, thick textured yarn. Choose a fleece that does not have any discoloured stains. All will have evidence of dirt, seeds, etc., which can be washed out. If in any doubt about a stain, ask your supplier as some cannot be removed.

SPINNING

Use a knee cloth. This will collect the dirt and seeds as they fall out during the spinning process.

Spinning 'in the grease' is the term used when wool is spun directly from the fleece with no washing, scouring and minimal sorting. The fleece contains lanolin which helps to keep the fibres together as you spin. Separate the fibres with your hands while spinning. Hold the wool in your left

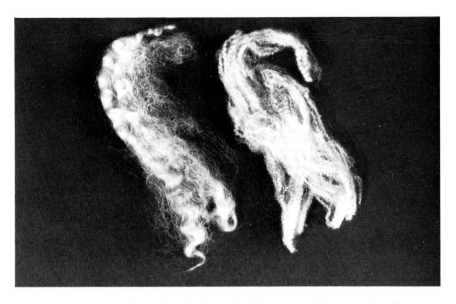

Border Leicester fleece (left) Merino fleece (right)

hand and with the right hand draw the fibres out. Arrange the fleece so that you feed the cut end of the staple into the spinner. (The staple is the length of each fibre.)

Sometimes it is difficult to remove all the grass seeds from the staple. Some will fall out as you separate the fibre, and the stubborn seeds can be removed during the washing process. The seed loses its 'grip' when wet and is also darker and easier to spot.

PLYING

For strength and durability, yarns can be plied together. When spinning a single strand, it is usual to turn the wheel in a clockwise direction. This is called the S-twist. When plying two or more strands together, turn the wheel in an anti-clockwise direction. This is called the Z-twist.

If a single strand is unattractively uneven, three strands plied together can improve the appearance. This is often more effective than two uneven strands plied together.

OVERSPINNING

Take care that you do not overspin and overply the wool. Severely overspun wool will be wire-like, hard to handle and brittle enough to break. A quick re-run through the spinning wheel in a Z-twist will help to remedy this. Likewise, overplied wool (two or more strands) can be put through the wheel in an S-twist.

Note Beginner's wool is often thick and lumpy, but it should not be discarded. When washed and knitted up employing a suitable tension, it has a charm of its own. If trying to spin a heavily textured yarn (thick or thin), a fine sewing thread can be used as the core or, alternatively, a single ply yarn. This makes the job quicker so you need to have the fleece ready to be spun on to the core. Mohair, silk, etc. can be incorporated in this manner.

WASHING

After spinning, the yarn is wound into hanks and tied loosely in at least two places with its own yarn or a contrast thread. There are two washing procedures depending on what you intend to do with the yarn.
Cold water wash   This allows the lanolin to remain in the yarn. Hot water would dissolve some of the lanolin, as would soaps, etc. The wool will not be as clean as if washed in warm water and soap but the retention of lanolin produces a water repellent quality. This type of wool is ideal for all-weather jumpers.

Soak the wool in cold water for 12 hours to loosen the dirt. Then rinse several times in cold water until water is clean. Remember, do not use soap or hot water. Unless the wool is to be dyed, it is a pity to wash out the lanolin. The clean 'sheepy' feel and smell of lanolin is part of the attraction of hand-spun yarns.

Washing for dyeing   The wool may be first soaked in cold water to loosen the dirt and rinsed several times in cold water. Then it needs several washes in hot water and dissolved soap or Softly. Remember not to subject the wool to sudden extremes of water temperature. After rinsing in water of a standard temperature, squeeze the wool dry. At this stage it can be rolled in a towel and patted dry or placed in the spin-dry cycle of the washing machine (never a wash or rinse).

At all times wool must be treated gently. Any rough or vigorous treatment when the wool is wet will result in shrinking, felting and loss of softness. Do not rub or wring the wool. Even water running from the tap on to the wool may affect it.

If you wish to dry the yarn so that it will hang straight, the skeins need to be gently weighted at the bottom. To prepare several hanks, you should ensure that each is of the same length, then rest a broom handle on the bottom of each hank. I have not found this necessary for hand-spun yarns. Dried gently in the breeze, the yarn will straighten, but not as uniformly as with a weight. The weighted method of straightening yarn is ideal for unravelled yarn which is full of kinks which will produce an uneven texture when re-knitted.

I have not found that sunlight affects the undyed yarns at all. Dyed yarns should, however, be dried in the shade unless their colourfastness is assured. Do not dry hand-spun yarn or garments in a drier.

PREPARATION FOR DYEING

Vegetable dyeing is a relatively simple operation. For the small amount of preparation, the results can be outstanding and, needless to say, very rewarding. You can dye white (cream) fleece as well as the various tones of 'black' fleece. The finer the fleece, the subtler the colour. The very fine Merino fleece will produce delicate shades while Border Leicester yarns will hold strong colours.

The yarn must be thoroughly washed and free of all trace of lanolin, grease and dirt. The next step is the mordanting process. Some vegetable dyes work on the yarn without the aid of a mordant, but until you have experimented yourself, it is safer to consider this step as essential to the dyeing process.

A mordant prepares the wool to accept the dye. Mordants are available in powder form from chemists, the basic mordants being alum, chrome, tin, iron and copper. Sometimes cream of tartar is added to the mordant bath to help brighten the final colour. Iron, on the other hand, tends to dull or 'sadden' the colour. Different mordants are able to extract different colours from the same dye-bath. For example, yarn treated with four different mordants but placed in the same dye-bath of *Euc. Macrocarpa* leaves will show four different colours, ranging from orange to dark grey.

Enamel, glass or stainless steel vessels must be used. Iron and aluminium pots, etc. may act as a mordant themselves. Keep these vessels for mordanting and dyeing. Don't use them for cooking later.

Once again, treat the yarn gently. Do not subject it to sudden extreme water temperatures. If adding more water to the mordant or dye-bath, ensure that it is of the same temperature.

Mix the mordant well with a small amount of water and then make sure it is well dissolved in the larger amount of water. Uneven mordanting of the yarn will cause uneven dyeing. Ideally, rain water should be used, but I have obtained good results with town water.

Method

Alum: Potassium aluminium sulphate (perhaps the most common of all mordants)·
85 gm (3 oz) alum
28 gm (1 oz) cream of tartar
0.45 kg (1 lb) wool
18 litres (4 gal) water
Dissolve alum and cream of tartar in a small amount of water and then mix thoroughly in 18 litres of water. Immerse yarn in the water and keep

submerged. Heat gently but never allow to boil. Simmer gently for one hour. Leave wool in mordant bath overnight. Squeeze dry, roll loosely in a towel and store in a plastic bag in a cool dry place. Yarn may be dyed immediately, but if kept damp for several days, better results will be achieved. Rinse mordanted wool well before dyeing.

Chrome: Potassium di-chromate

7 to 14 gm (¼ – ½ oz) chrome (less chrome for fine wool)

0.45 kg (1 lb) wool

18–20 litres (4–4½ gal) water

Dissolve chrome in the large amount of water, then follow the same procedure as for alum. Chrome, however, is very sensitive to light so keep yarn submerged and a lid on the vessel. Keep the chrome-mordanted yarn in a dark place. Dye directly after mordanting for the best results.

Iron: Ferrous sulphate

14 g (½ oz) iron

28 gm (1 oz) cream of tartar

0.45 kg (1 lb) wool

18–20 litres (4–4½ gal) water

The procedure with iron is reversed. Dye the yarn first before mordanting. Simmer yarn in dye for 30 minutes. Remove yarn and add iron and cream of tartar dissolved in a little water. Mix well and then add yarn. Bring gently to a simmer for 10–15 minutes. Rinse thoroughly. It is desirable to use a separate vessel for iron mordanting as the iron can affect subsequent dyeing.

Tin: Stannous chloride

7–14 gm (¼ – ½ oz) tin

56 gm (2 oz) cream of tartar

0.45 kg (1 lb) wool

18–20 litres (4–4½ gal) water

Dissolve tin and cream of tartar separately and add to the large amount of water. Simmer gently for a few minutes. Let bath cool and add damp yarn. Reheat gradually and simmer for 30 minutes. Rinse well and use as needed.

Tin is not generally used as a mordant, but rather as an additive towards the end of the dyeing process. A small amount of dissolved tin crystals added to a dye-bath will help brighten the colour. Tin tends to make the wool feel harsh and brittle. Wash wool in soapy water after mordanting and rinse until clear.

Copper: Copper sulphate

7–14 gm (¼ – ½ oz) copper

0.45 kg (1 lb) wool

18–20 litres (4–4½ gal) water

Add dissolved copper crystals to the large amount of water and simmer gently for a few minutes. Cool the water and add the yarn. Reheat gradually and simmer for 10 minutes. Cool and rinse yarn. Yarn can be used immediately. Copper may also be used as an additive with other mordants towards the end of a dye-bath.

The choice of mordant may seem confusing. Just remember that each will produce a different colour from the same dye-bath. Below you will find some of the vegetable matter which can be used in conjunction with specific mordants to obtain a certain colour.

DYEING

My inclination is to use solely Australian flora. If this is your intention, please respect rules regarding the trees and bushes. Where necessary, obtain permission to pick leaves, etc.

Keep a record of each dyeing session and dye sufficient quantities of wool as it is hard to match the same colour at another session. Your records should show:

1 Date of plant collection and location
2 Date of the dyeing session
3 Type of plant and which part (leaves, bark, etc.) and quantity
4 Type of wool and quantity

5 Name of mordant and quantity
6 Vessels used
7 Other relevant points, e.g. results, etc.

You can place the damp wool in the bath with the vegetable matter. However, better results are generally achieved if the dye is first extracted from the leaves, etc. and the matter is removed before immersing the yarn. It is also preferable to place leaves loosely in the dye vessel, rather than enclosing them in a fabric bag.

Some dye materials release their colour readily while others require longer periods of simmering.

When the dye matter is collected is important. The plants will give different results if picked during a drought or after rainfall. Try to find pest-free vegetable matter. Dry the leaves, flowers, berries, etc. before using. When ready to use, tear up or crush the vegetable matter and soak overnight in sufficient water. The quality of vegetable matter may vary from species to species. For example, to obtain red from the leaves of *Euc. Cinerea*, a large quantity of leaves is needed.

After dyeing, several rinses are needed. Dry in a breezy spot away from direct sunlight.

Many of the colours attained will be colourfast. To test for colour-fastness, place several long strands of dyed yarn half in and half out of a box with a lid. Ensure that the box is lightproof and place it in a sunny spot for a few days or longer. On comparison, it will be obvious whether or not that particular dyeing process was colourfast. Most dyes will not run during washing. Always avoid harsh detergents with bleaches.

After dyed yarn is dry, wind it into balls for easier use.

OVERDYEING

The yarn is dyed in one dye-bath first, rinsed and dried (or left damp). The damp wool is then placed into a different dye-bath and the dyeing procedure repeated.

COLOURS

Below are a few of the colours obtainable from native flora and various mordants. Amounts of dry vegetable matter will vary according to the depth of the colour you desire.

Cootamundra Wattle (*Acacia Baileyana*)
Leaves and stems
   alum — yellow
   chrome — dark gold, pink-tan, gold-green
   copper — dark green
   tin, cream of tartar and oxalic acid — bright yellow-gold
   alum, tin and tannic acid — orange
Flowers
   alum — yellow

Coast Banksia (*Banksia Integrifolia*)
Leaves
   alum — lemon-yellow

Bottle-brush (*Callistemon Citrinus* [syn. *C. Lanceolatus*])
Leaves
   alum — yellow-fawn
   iron — grey
   chrome — dull gold

Mangrove (*Calophyllum Irophyllum*)
Leaves
   alum — fawn
   tin — gold
   copper — brown
   iron — green

Mealy Stringybark (*Euc. Cinerea*)
Leaves
   alum — red
   chrome — brown-tan
   no mordant — pink-brown
Bark
   alum — fawn-brown
   chrome — brown
   iron — brown

Mottlecah (*Euc. Macrocarpa*)
Leaves
   alum — orange
   tin — yellow
   copper — fawn
   iron — dark grey

Lemon Scented (*Euc. Citriodora*)
Leaves
   alum — yellow-fawn
   no mordant — fawn-brown
Bark
   alum and acetic acid — yellow

Swamp Mahogany (*Euc. Robusta*)
Leaves
   alum — green-lemon

Sydney Blue Gum (*Euc. Saligna*)
Leaves
   alum — light tan
   tin — yellow
   copper — light brown
   iron — brown
   iron and copper — dark grey
   iron and tin — green

Grey Box (*Euc. Microcarpa*)
Leaves
   alum — lemon-yellow
   tin — yellow
   copper — fawn-green
   iron — dark grey
   iron and copper — black
   iron and tin — green
   chrome — fawn-tan

She-oak (*Casuarina Cunninghamiana*)
Leaves
   alum — gold-lemon
   copper — green-fawn
   iron — grey

Detailed instructions for Koala and Possum jumpers

As hand-spun yarns may vary greatly among individual spinners and with different qualities of fleece, you may have to adapt the Koala and Possum patterns to suit your particular hand-spun yarn.

There are a few basic steps to follow to design your own garment.

1 Knit a swatch using your hand-spun yarn. This should be worked in the main colour and in the main stitch pattern (usually stocking stitch). Choose a pair of suitable needles and cast on 20 stitches. Knit 15 to 20 rows and judge if the quality is suitable for your intended garment.

Is it too hard or stiff to the touch? If so, use a size larger needles, and if necessary, keep progressing up a size until you are satisfied with the feel and look of your knitted fabric. Is it too loose and open? If so, use a size (or two sizes, etc.) smaller needles.

The knitted fabric should feel supple and soft, yet still retain its stitch shape and row alignment. You can, of course, vary this rule if you prefer a special effect in your knitting.

Always mark with a coloured thread at each end of the row where the change in needle size occurs.

2 Once you have decided which size needles suit your hand-spun yarn, the tension can be worked out. Lie the swatch flat on a hard surface. With a rule and pins, mark off 10 cm from the edge along a row. Count the number of stitches. Do this several times along different rows until you are satisfied that you have a correct count.

Now you can work out how many stitches are needed for a required measurement.

Do the same to work out how many rows make 10 cm. This information will be useful when you wish to prepare a graph of your jumper and to incorporate a design.

3 The measurements on the pattern pieces below can be changed to suit your requirements.

Koala jumper

NECK

The neck opening on both front and back is a third of the width. Avoid making the front neckline square by shaping the neck edge. To do this, determine how many stitches make up the third. Half of this number can be cast off in the centre at 55 cm from the beginning. The other half of the stitches will be used up on both sides of the neck edge to form the shaping. The shaping is usually formed by decreasing one stitch at neck edge every alternate row, then continuing straight until required length is

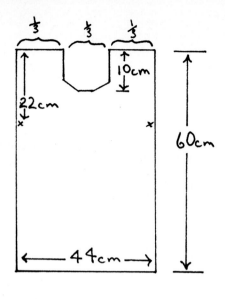

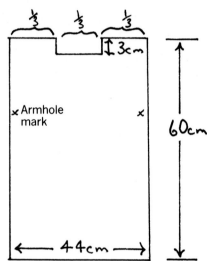

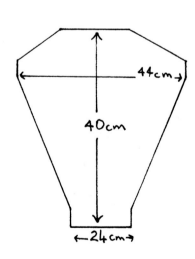

reached. Cast off. Join yarn to remaining stitches and complete other side to correspond.

The back neck is very straightforward. At 57 cm, cast off centre one-third of stitches. Knit without shaping for 3 cm. Cast off. Join yarn to remaining stitches and complete other side to correspond.

SLEEVES

You need to work out from your tension swatch the maximum number of stitches for the final width and the number of rows for the desired length of sleeve. Thus, you can work out a comfortable increase from the cuff basque for the sleeve shaping. The usual method is to increase 1 stitch at each end of every fourth (or sixth or eighth) row until the required number of stitches has been reached. Then continue straight until desired length.

There are two ways of completing the sleeve top.

1 To shape the sleeve top, work out a convenient number of stitches to cast off for the next 6, 8 or 10 rows. Any remaining stitches are cast off at the end. This gives sufficient 'rise' to the sleeve top for a comfortable fit.

2 Once increase shaping is complete, knit straight for required length and cast off loosely.

RIBBING

Choose needles two or three sizes smaller than those required for the body of the jumper.

NECKBAND

Sew up one shoulder. This eliminates the need to use a set of four needles, although you can alter this direction to suit your preference. With ribbing sized needles, pick up, fairly closely together, but loosely, a comfortable number of stitches. This should be an even number for a rib of K.1, P.1. Don't skimp on the number of stitches for the neckband, otherwise you may find the neck opening will be too tight. Knit 10 cm of rib and then cast off very loosely in rib, perhaps even changing to a larger needle for this purpose. Sew up shoulder, join neckband, fold it in half and slip-stitch to the inside.

GRAPH

If the tension of your test swatch matches the tension of the Koala jumper, then you can follow the graph as shown. However, if you had to knit more (or less) stitches to make up 10 cm, then the Koala graph needs to be adjusted otherwise the shape will be distorted. This involves drawing up a graph of the exact number of stitches and rows of your jumper and then sketching in your version of the Koala.

DYEING

The green yarn in the Koala jumper was obtained by dyeing natural white fleece with gum leaves. A mordant of copper sulphate was used. Jean K. Carman's *Dyemaking with Eucalypts* (Rigby, 1978) is a very useful book which deals efficiently and clearly with all the necessary steps as well as indicating how to obtain a great variety of colour from the humble gum tree.

I adapted her instructions to obtain my small quantity of green yarn. I used 7 gm (1 teaspoon) of copper sulphate, 8 litres of water, 500 gm of dried iron-bark gum (*E. paniculata*) leaves and 200 gm spun yarn.

1 Use only enamel or stainless steel pots as aluminium, copper or iron pots may act as a mordant.

2 Prepare yarn for washing and dyeing by winding it into hanks and tying loosely in two places to prevent tangling.

3 Tear up dried gum leaves and soak in water overnight. Then simmer gently for at least 1 hour. Strain off leaves and keep dye-bath.

4 Wash spun fleece in soapy hot water to remove any trace of grease and dirt. Yarn may be dried away from direct sun or left damp if you are able to complete all processes at one time.

5   Dissolve copper sulphate crystals in a little water, then add 8 litres of water and bring to a simmer for 10 minutes. Allow to cool slightly, add damp wool, reheat slowly and simmer gently for 10 minutes.
6   Rinse yarn well in warm to hot water.
7   Add yarn to dye-bath. Repeat slowly and simmer gently for 10 minutes.
8   Remove yarn from dye-bath and rinse well in warm to hot water. Allow to dry in the shade.
9   Never subject the yarn to sudden extremes of water temperature as this will felt and shrink the wool. Wool should not be allowed to boil vigorously, but should be kept at a gentle simmer. Boiling will harden and cause deterioration of the fibre.

Possum jumper

YOKE

The measurement for the yoke is taken from wrist, along arm, across shoulders, along second arm to wrist. The graph of the yoke is based on half of this measurement. The width is determined by measuring from shoulder to underarm and adding 4 cm. The neckline should measure 20 cm wide and 10 cm deep.

BODY

This piece is a rectangle measuring from underarm to length desired including the ribbed band. The width will be half of the chest measurement plus 4 cm for ease of fit.

GUSSETS

These are small knitted squares of stocking stitch. They are sewn in where yoke/sleeve joins the body at right angles and help to eliminate strain on the seams. Knit two gussets 5 cm square using same needles as for body.

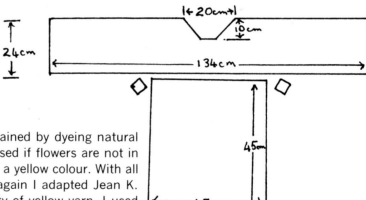

DYEING

The yellow colour in the Possum jumper was obtained by dyeing natural white fleece with wattle flowers. Leaves may be used if flowers are not in season. Alternatively, passionfruit leaves also give a yellow colour. With all three dye materials, the mordant is alum. Once again I adapted Jean K. Carman's instructions to obtain my small quantity of yellow yarn. I used 50 gm (2 tablespoons) alum, 20 gm (1 teaspoon) cream of tartar, 8 litres of water, 400 gm of dried wattle flowers and 200 gm of spun yarn.
1   Use only enamel, glass or stainless steel pots as aluminium and iron pots will act as a mordant as well.
2   Prepare yarn for washing and dyeing by winding into hanks and loosely tying in two places.
3   Soak dried and torn up flowers (or leaves) in water overnight. Then simmer gently for 1 hour. Strain off flowers (or leaves) and keep dye-bath.
4   Using another pot, dissolve alum and cream of tartar in a little hot water and add to the 8 litres.
5   Submerge the washed damp wool in solution and simmer gently for an hour, stirring wool occasionally. Cool and allow to stand in mordant overnight. Squeeze, dry and roll in clean towel to store, if necessary.
6   Rinse mordanted wool before dyeing.
7   Add yarn to dye-bath and simmer gently till desired colour is achieved.
8   Remove wool from dye-bath and rinse in hot to warm water several times. Allow to dry in the shade.
9   When dry, wind into balls.

Bibliography

Blombery, Alec M., *What Wildflower Is That?*, Sydney, Paul Hamlyn, 1972.

Carman, Jean K., *Dyemaking with Eucalypts*, Adelaide, Rigby, 1978.

Cox, Truda, *Beginning Spinning*, Sydney, Wentworth Books, 1976.

Duncan, Molly, *Spin Your Own Wool*, Wellington, A. H. & A. W. Reed, 1968.

Edwards, Bruce, *Kookaburras & Kingfishers*, Melbourne, Lansdowne Press, 1972.

Frith, H. J., Cons.Ed., *Complete Book of Australian Birds*, Sydney, Reader's Digest, 1976.

Jeffs, Angela, Cons.Ed., *Wild Knitting*, New York, A. & W. Publishers Inc., 1979.

Lammer, Jutta, *The Book of Needlecraft*, London, Ward Lock, 1973.

McCarthy, F. D., *Australian Aboriginal Culture*, Canberra, Aust. Government Publishing Service, 1973.

McCarthy, F. D., *Australian Aboriginal Decorative Art*, Sydney, The Australian Museum, 1974.

Millard, Nancy, *The Handspun Crochet Book*, Sydney, A. H. & A. W. Reed, 1979.

Rogers, F. J. C., *Growing Australian Native Plants*, Melbourne, Thomas Nelson (Australia), 1971.

The Handweavers and Spinners Guild of Victoria, *Dyemaking with Australian Flora*, Adelaide, Rigby, 1974.

Wilson, Sherry, *Creative Knitting*, Sydney, A. H. & A. W. Reed, 1979.

Other

Aboriginal Arts, Aboriginal Prehistory, Bark Painting, Sydney, Aboriginal Arts & Crafts.

Golden Hands, Parts 14, 26, 27, London, Marshall Cavendish, 1975.

In the Wild with Harry Butler, Sydney, Australian Broadcasting Commission, 1977.

Mon Tricot Knitting Dictionary, New Edition, France, Jean-Louis Perrier, 1979.

Oenpelli Paintings on Bark, Sydney, Aboriginal Arts Board of the Australia Council, 1973.

The Living Bush, Sydney, Women's Weekly, Australian Consolidated Press.